www.rusi.org

# Future NATO: Adapting to New Realities

Edited by John Andreas Olsen

# Royal United Services Institute for Defence and Security Studies

Future NATO: Adapting to New Realities
First published 2020

Whitehall Papers series

Series Editor: Professor Malcolm Chalmers
Editor: Emma De Angelis

RUSI is a Registered Charity (No. 210639)
ISBN [978-0-367-53472-1]

Published on behalf of the Royal United Services Institute for Defence and Security Studies
by
Routledge Journals, an imprint of Taylor & Francis, 4 Park Square, Milton Park, Abingdon OX14 4RN

Cover Image: Illustration of NATO headquarters taken after a meeting between the Belgian prime minister and the NATO secretary-general in the new building of NATO headquarters in Brussels, 22 June 2018. *Courtesy of PA Images/Benoit Doppagne*

**SUBSCRIPTIONS**
Please send subscription order to:

**USA/Canada:** Taylor & Francis Inc., Journals Department, 325 Chestnut Street, 8th Floor, Philadelphia, PA 19106 USA

**UK/Rest of World:** Routledge Journals, T&F Customer Services, T&F Informa UK Ltd, Sheepen Place, Colchester, Essex, C03 0LP UK

# Contents

## About the Editor

**John Andreas Olsen** is a Colonel in the Royal Norwegian Air Force, currently assigned to London as Defence Attaché to the UK and Ireland. He is a non-resident Senior Fellow of the Mitchell Institute of Aerospace Studies, Washington, DC. His previous assignments include tours as Director of Security Analyses in the Norwegian Ministry of Defence; Deputy Commander and Chief of the NATO Advisory Team at the NATO Headquarters, Sarajevo; Dean of the Norwegian Defence University College; and Head of the College's Division for Strategic Studies. Olsen is a graduate of the German Command and Staff College and has served both as liaison officer to the German Operational Command in Potsdam and as military assistant to the Norwegian Embassy in Berlin. He has a Doctorate in History and International Relations from De Montfort University, a Master's degree in Contemporary Literature from the University of Warwick and a Master's degree in English from the University of Trondheim. He was a Visiting Professor at the Swedish National Defence University from 2008 to 2019.

Dr Olsen has lectured worldwide, received several awards and published many books. His recent publications have included *Airpower Reborn: The Strategic Concepts of John Warden and John Boyd* (2015); *NATO and the North Atlantic: Revitalising Collective Defence* (2017); *Airpower Applied: US, NATO and Israeli Combat Experience* (2017); *The Routledge Handbook of Air Power* (2018); and *Security in Northern Europe: Deterrence, Defence and Dialogue* (2018).

## About the Authors

**James Henry Bergeron** is Political Advisor (POLAD) to the Commander, NATO Allied Maritime Command in Northwood, UK, and was previously the POLAD to Naval Striking and Support Forces NATO. His operational tours as POLAD include Joint Task Force Lebanon (2006), the Russia–Georgia conflict (2008) and NATO's Combined Joint Task Force Operation *Unified Protector* (2011). He is regularly consulted on NATO political affairs and was one of the drafters of the Alliance Maritime Strategy. A retired Commander in the US Navy Reserve and former law professor, he taught EU and international law for 15 years and has published articles and book chapters on international law, anti-trust law and security studies. Bergeron holds a JD from Syracuse University and an LLM from the London School of Economics. He is Honorary Professor of International Relations at the University of Plymouth.

**Keith Blount** is the Commander of NATO's Allied Maritime Command. As such, he is NATO's principal maritime adviser and has operational command of NATO's Standing Naval Force. He joined the Royal Navy in 1984 as a helicopter pilot and has blended his aviation experience with assignments at sea and in command. He sailed in NATO Task Groups during Operation *Sharp Guard* and Operation *Active Endeavour* and worked together with NATO when serving in the Combined Maritime Forces and EU NAVFOR. He has commanded three warships, including the helicopter carrier HMS *Ocean*, and was the Iraqi Maritime Task Group Commander during Operation *Telic*. More recently, he was the UK's Maritime Component Commander, spanning operations in Syria and Iraq. His staff appointments have included three periods in the Ministry of Defence; his last London assignment was as Military Assistant to the Vice Chief of the Defence Staff. He holds a Master's degree in Defence Studies from King's College London.

**Heinrich Brauss** retired from the German armed forces in July 2018 and holds the rank of lieutenant general. He was NATO's Assistant Secretary General for Defence Policy and Planning from 2013 to 2018, having joined the International Staff of NATO in 2007 as Deputy Assistant Secretary General for Policy and Planning. Prior to joining NATO, he served at the EU, first in the EU Military Staff as Assistant Chief of Staff,

Operations and Exercises Division, and then as Director of the Civilian/ Military Cell and the EU Operations Centre. He commanded an armoured brigade in Potsdam, Germany, and served as Chief of Staff at Headquarters Stabilisation Force (SFOR), Sarajevo. General Brauss first gained international experience as a member of the staff of the German Military Representative in the Military Committee of NATO and EU/WEU in Brussels. He also served as Branch Chief in the Planning and Advisory Staff to the former German Minister of Defence, Volker Rühe.

**Philip M Breedlove** served as Supreme Allied Commander, Europe and Commander of US European Command from 2013 to 2016. In 2012 and 2013, he was Commander, US Air Forces, Europe; Commander, US Air Forces, Africa; and Commander, Headquarters Allied Air Command, Ramstein. General Breedlove has served in a variety of senior leadership positions for the USAF, including as Vice Director for Strategic Plans and Policy on the Joint Staff; Deputy Chief of Staff for Operations, Plans and Requirements for the USAF Headquarters; and Vice Chief of Staff of the USAF. He earned a Bachelor's degree in Civil Engineering from the Georgia Institute of Technology, a Master's degree in Aeronautical Technology from Arizona State University and a Master's degree in National Security Studies from the National War College. He is a member of the board of directors of the Atlantic Council and is a distinguished professor at the Sam Nunn School of International Affairs at Georgia Tech.

**Corentin Brustlein** is the Director of the Security Studies Center at the French Institute of International Relations (IFRI) in Paris. His work focuses on nuclear and conventional deterrence, arms control, military balances and US and French defence policies. Before assuming his current position in 2015, he was a Research Fellow at IFRI and a lecturer at the University of Lyon. He has been the lead editor of IFRI's *Proliferation Papers* since 2014 and currently serves on the UN Secretary-General's Advisory Board on Disarmament Matters. His most recent publications include 'The Erosion of Strategic Stability and The Future of Arms Control in Europe' (2018) and 'Entry Operations and the Future of Strategic Autonomy' (2017). He has co-authored a book on the erosion of Western air supremacy, titled *La suprématie aérienne en péril. Menaces et contre-stratégies à l'horizon 2030* (2014). He holds a PhD in Political Science from the Jean Moulin University of Lyon.

**Malcolm Chalmers** is RUSI's Deputy Director-General and oversees the Institute's research programmes. His own research focuses on UK defence, foreign and security policy. His recent publications have included studies on the Ministry of Defence's 2019 spending settlement;

the 'rules-based international system'; nuclear arms control; Brexit and European security; the UK's Modernising Defence Programme review; prospects for, and implications of, a war in Korea; the UK and the North Atlantic; and future nuclear threats to the UK. Chalmers was a member of the consultative panel for both the 2010 and 2015 Strategic Defence and Security Reviews. During 2006 and 2007, he was a Senior Special Adviser in the Foreign Commonwealth Office to Foreign Secretaries Jack Straw MP and Margaret Beckett MP. He has been an Adviser to Parliament's Joint Committee on the National Security Strategy since 2012 and is an honorary professor at the University of Exeter's Strategy and Security Institute.

**Jeffrey Edmonds** is an expert on Russia and Eurasia at the Center for Naval Analyses. His research focuses on the Russian military, foreign policy, threat perceptions and information operations. He most recently served as Director for Russia on the National Security Council (NSC) and Acting Senior Director for Russia during the 2017 presidential transition. While on the NSC, Edmonds advised the president and his senior staff on Russia-related national security topics that included the Ukraine and Syria crises, Russian military developments and foreign policy. Prior to his tenure on the NSC, he was a senior Eurasian military analyst with the CIA. Edmonds served in the Army both on active duty and in the Reserves for 22 years, with tours in both Afghanistan and Iraq. He holds an MPA from Harvard's Kennedy School of Government, an MA from Boston University in Religious Studies and a BS from the US Military Academy.

**Svein Efjestad** became Policy Director at the Norwegian Ministry of Defence (MoD) in 2013. He joined the MoD in 1981 after having completed his Master's degree in Political Science at the University of Oslo and spending a brief period at the Norwegian Institute of International Relations (NUPI). Efjestad has held different positions in the MoD and served in the Norwegian delegation to NATO from 1986 to 1990. From 1995 to 2013, he served as Director-General for Security Policy at the MoD and participated in several national and international committees dealing with different security policy issues. In his current position, Efjestad is primarily engaged in policy planning, support to security policy research, Nordic Defence Cooperation and bilateral defence and security issues. He is also the Chairman of the Norwegian Coast Guard Council.

**Andrea Kendall-Taylor** is a Senior Fellow and Director of the Transatlantic Security Program at the Center for a New American Security (CNAS). Prior to joining CNAS, she served for eight years as a senior intelligence officer. From 2015 to 2018, she was Deputy National Intelligence Officer for Russia and

Eurasia at the National Intelligence Council in the Office of the Director of National Intelligence. Prior to that, she was a Senior Analyst at the CIA, where she worked on Russia and Eurasia, the political dynamics of autocracies and the decline of democracy. Dr Kendall-Taylor received her BA in Politics from Princeton University and her PhD in Political Science from the University of California, Los Angeles. She is also an adjunct professor at Georgetown University's School of Foreign Service.

**Ziya Meral** is a Senior Resident Fellow at the British Army's Centre for Historical Analysis and Conflict Research based at the Royal Military Academy Sandhurst, a Senior Associate Fellow at RUSI, and the Director of the Centre on Religion and Global Affairs, based in London, Accra and Beirut. He is a frequent commentator in the British and international media and has presented testimony before the House of Commons' Foreign Affairs Committee, as well as lectures at the NATO Defence College, US State Department and EU Commission. Dr Meral holds a PhD in Politics from the University of Cambridge, an MSc in Sociology from the London School of Economics, and a BA (Hons) in Theology from Brunel University. He is the author of *How Violence Shapes Religion: Belief and Conflict in Africa and Middle East* (2019).

**Janka Oertel** is the Director of the Asia Programme at the European Council on Foreign Relations. She previously worked as a Senior Fellow in the Asia Program at the German Marshall Fund (GMF) of the US's Berlin office. Prior to joining the GMF, she served as a Programme Director at the Körber Foundation's Berlin office, where she was responsible for the Berlin Foreign Policy Forum as well as the Asia activities of the foundation's International Affairs Department. She holds a PhD from the University of Jena, was a Visiting Fellow at the German Institute for International and Security Affairs (SWP Berlin) and worked at UN Headquarters as a Carlo Schmid Fellow. She has published various works on topics related to security in the Asia-Pacific region, Chinese foreign policy, 5G and emerging technologies and UN peacekeeping, including *China and the United Nations: Chinese UN Policy in the Areas of Peace and Development under Hu Jintao* (2014).

**Frans Osinga** is an Air Commodore in the Royal Netherlands Air Force, and Professor of War Studies, Head of the Military Operational Art and Science Section, and Chair of the War Studies Programme at the Netherlands Defence Academy. He teaches courses on coercive diplomacy, contemporary warfare and strategy, and peace operations in the BA War Studies programme and the MA Strategic Studies programme. Osinga is also the Special Chair in War Studies at Leiden University. He is an F-16 pilot and a graduate of the Netherlands Advanced Staff Course and has studied at the USAF Air University. His positions include a tour as the MoD Research Fellow at the Clingendael Institute. He wrote his PhD dissertation at Leiden University on the strategic thought of John Boyd. He has published more than 60 articles and co-edited books, including *Military Adaptation in Afghanistan* (2013), *Targeting: The Challenges of Modern Warfare* (2015) and *Winning Without Killing* (2017).

**Tim Sweijs** is the Director of Research at The Hague Centre for Strategic Studies (HCSS). He is the initiator, creator and author of numerous studies, methodologies and tools for horizon scanning, early warning, conflict analysis, national security risk assessment, and strategy and capability development. His main research interest concerns the changing character of contemporary conflict. Dr Sweijs is a Senior Research Fellow at the Netherlands Defence Academy and an Affiliate at the Center for International Strategy, Technology and Policy in the Sam Nunn School of International Affairs at Georgia Tech. He also serves as an Adviser on Technology, Conflict and National Interest to the UK Government's Stabilisation Unit. Sweijs holds degrees in War Studies (PhD, MA), International Relations (MSc) and Philosophy (BA) from King's College London and the University of Amsterdam. He is currently working on two book projects, titled *The Conduct of War* and *Deterrence Revisited: Insights from Theory and Practice for the 2020s*.

**Rolf Tamnes** is a Professor at the Norwegian Institute for Defence Studies. He served as the Institute's Director for 16 years (1996–2012), as head of the international research programme 'Geopolitics in the High North' (2008–12) and as Adjunct Professor at the University of Oslo (1995–2009). Tamnes has been a Visiting Fellow at the Center for Strategic and International Studies (2005–06) and St Antony's College, Oxford (2014). He has also been a public policy scholar at the Woodrow Wilson International Center. Most recently, he chaired the Expert Commission on Norwegian Security and Defence Policy, appointed by the Norwegian MoD, and served as a core member of the Afghanistan Inquiry Committee, appointed by the Norwegian government. He has published many books, including co-authored works such as *Common or Divided Security? German and Norwegian Perspectives on Euro-Atlantic Security* (2014) and *Geopolitics and Security in the Arctic: Regional Dynamics in a Global World* (2014).

**Alexander R Vershbow** has been a Distinguished Fellow at the Atlantic Council's Scowcroft Center for Strategy and Security in Washington, DC, since 2017. Ambassador Vershbow was the Deputy Secretary General of NATO from 2012 to 2016 and was centrally involved in shaping the

Alliance's response to Russia's aggression against Ukraine. Prior to his post at NATO, he served for three years as the US Assistant Secretary of Defense for International Security Affairs, overseeing US policy towards Europe, Eurasia, the Middle East and Africa. Vershbow served as US ambassador to NATO (1998–2001), to the Russian Federation (2001–05), and to the Republic of Korea (2005–08). He also held numerous senior policy positions in Washington, including as Senior Director for European Affairs at the NSC (1994–97) and State Department Director of Soviet Union Affairs (1988–91). Vershbow holds degrees in International Relations and Russian Studies from Yale and Columbia Universities. He is a member of the Council on Foreign Relations.

# Acronyms and Abbreviations

| | |
|---|---|
| **A2/AD** | Anti-access/area denial |
| **AI** | Artificial intelligence |
| **ASAT** | Anti-satellite |
| **ASW** | Anti-submarine warfare |
| **AU** | African Union |
| **AWACS** | Airborne Warning and Control System |
| **BCT** | Brigade combat team |
| **C2** | Command and control |
| **C4ISR** | Command, control, communications, computers, intelligence, surveillance and reconnaissance |
| **CARD** | Coordinated Annual Review on Defence (EU) |
| **CBRN** | Chemical, biological, radiological and nuclear |
| **CCP** | Chinese Communist Party |
| **CEMA** | Cyber and electromagnetic activities |
| **CFE** | Conventional Forces Europe |
| **CMC** | Central Military Commission (China) |
| **CSDP** | Common Security and Defence Policy |
| **DCA** | Dual-capable aircraft |
| **EAPC** | Euro-Atlantic Partnership Council |
| **EDF** | European Defence Fund |
| **EDI** | European Deterrence Initiative |
| **EFP** | Enhanced Forward Presence |
| **ERI** | European Reassurance Initiative |
| **EUFOR** | European Force Mission – Bosnia and Herzegovina |
| **FONOPS** | Freedom of navigation operations |
| **GCC** | Gulf Cooperation Council |
| **GEC** | Global Engagement Center (US State Department) |
| **GIUK gap** | Greenland – Iceland – UK gap |
| **ICBM** | Intercontinental ballistic missile |
| **ICI** | Istanbul Cooperation Initiative |
| **INF** | Intermediate-Range Nuclear Forces Treaty |
| **ISIS** | Islamic State of Iraq and Syria (also known as Daesh) |
| **ISR** | Intelligence, surveillance and reconnaissance |
| **JFC** | Joint Force Command |
| **JSEC** | Joint Support and Enabling Command |
| **MARCOM** | Allied Maritime Command |

| | |
|---|---|
| **MD** | Mediterranean Dialogue |
| **MENA** | Middle East and North Africa |
| **MIRV** | Multiple independently targeted re-entry vehicles |
| **MND-SE** | Multinational Division Southeast |
| **NACC** | North Atlantic Cooperation Council |
| **NAVFOR** | Naval Force Operation (EU) |
| **NCS** | NATO Command Structure |
| **NPT** | Nuclear Non-Proliferation Treaty |
| **NRC** | NATO–Russia Council |
| **NRF** | NATO Response Force |
| **NRI** | NATO Readiness Initiative |
| **NSD–S Hub** | NATO Strategic Direction – South Hub |
| **OODA** | Observe, orient, decide, act |
| **OSG** | Operation *Sea Guardian* |
| **PESCO** | Permanent Structured Cooperation |
| **PfP** | Partnership for Peace |
| **PKK** | Kurdistan Workers' Party |
| **PLA** | People's Liberation Army |
| **PLAA** | PLA Army |
| **PLAN** | PLA Navy |
| **PLASSF** | PLA Strategic Support Force |
| **RMA** | Revolution in military affairs |
| **SACEUR** | Supreme Allied Commander, Europe |
| **SACLANT** | Supreme Allied Commander, Atlantic |
| **SALT** | Strategic Arms Limitation Talks |
| **SEAD** | Suppression of enemy air defence |
| **SIPRI** | Stockholm International Peace Research Institute |
| **SNMG** | Standing NATO Maritime Group |
| **STO** | Science and Technology Organization (NATO) |
| **USAREUR** | US Army in Europe |
| **USEUCOM** | US European Command |
| **UUV** | Unmanned underwater vehicle |
| **VJTF** | Very High Readiness Joint Task Force |
| **YPG** | Kurdish People's Protection Units |

# Preface

*Future NATO* completes a trilogy of security and defence publications in RUSI's Whitehall Paper series. The first – *NATO and the North Atlantic: Revitalising Collective Defence* (2017) – focuses on the renewed importance of the transatlantic bond from US, UK and Norwegian perspectives. The second – *Security in Northern Europe: Deterrence, Defence and Dialogue* (2018) – takes a broader view, analysing challenges confronting the 12 Northern Group countries, the US and Canada. Both papers were publicised through comprehensive outreach programmes and presented at seminars in 25 countries, with the objective of encouraging an informed and open debate on national policy and international relations with emphasis on the northern region. That debate served as input for this third Whitehall Paper.

*Future NATO: Adapting to New Realities* (2020) expands the view further, identifying key themes that the Alliance and its partners must examine and address to remain relevant in the decades to come. As NATO recently celebrated 70 years of 'credible deterrence and collective defence', this paper focuses on the features of the current security and defence landscape, and on what NATO members should do, individually and together, to strengthen the organisation in order to meet present and future challenges.

I would like to thank all the authors of this volume for their contributions. It has been a true pleasure working with such a distinguished group of experts. I am once again in debt to freelance editor Margaret S MacDonald for valuable editorial advice and to Professor Mats Berdal of King's College London, Professor Peter Roberts of RUSI and Colonel (ret.) Per Erik Solli of Nord University for their support in the development of all three publications. I am also grateful to RUSI for another round of excellent cooperation, with special thanks to the Director of Publications, Dr Emma De Angelis.

**John Andreas Olsen**
March 2020

# FOREWORD

## TOD D WOLTERS

NATO is a political and military alliance whose principal task is to ensure the protection of the nearly 1 billion citizens of its member states and to promote security and stability in the North Atlantic area. The foundation of that principal task is our democratic value system.

My main priority as Supreme Allied Commander Europe, bar none, is to promote NATO's shared values of democracy, individual liberty and the rule of law. These values have held the Alliance together for more than 70 years, through the decades of the Cold War and since. They were the priority of General Dwight D Eisenhower and the other 17 commanders who have held this office before me, and so they will also remain my true north. Whenever there were internal disputes among NATO's constituent members – and there have been a few over the years – those core values ensured that we overcame disagreements and stood together when it mattered. Our shared values are fundamental to Alliance cohesion; they make the Article 5 commitment credible.

The importance of Article 5 cannot be emphasised strongly enough: all for one, one for all. This solidarity pact is essential to unity and its execution depends on NATO's two core tasks: credible deterrence and collective defence. That constancy of purpose is the reason we stand together in our response to revisionist Russia, international terrorism and a range of other challenges from near and afar.

Our operations, activities and exercises demonstrate that NATO is ready to act. The recent NATO Readiness Initiative is important. Equally important is the strengthening of NATO's command structure with the addition of the Joint Support and Enabling Command in Ulm, to improve mobility of forces across Europe, and the Joint Force Command in Norfolk, Virginia. The latter will offer high-end capabilities in the North Atlantic and open sea lines of communication across the high seas and far into the European High North, since NATO's area of responsibility stretches all the way to the North Pole.

Added to this, NATO's new military strategy fosters a culture of readiness that strengthens our ability to act when and where needed. It is the first time in decades that we have produced such guidance; it gives us the opportunity to go forward with a productive strategy. The strategy will guide Allied military decision-making and provide NATO's military authorities with a definitive policy reference. It defines the 'large picture' ends, ways and means and outlines the approach that we will take to neutralise near-peer competitors and exhaust the resources of international terror groups. The main components are to strengthen capabilities and improve speed: speed of decision-making and speed of action on the ground, in the air and at sea. The NATO Readiness Initiative, the strengthening of the command structure to make it fit for purpose and the new military strategy demonstrate that NATO is constantly adapting to new challenges.

The success of NATO depends on hardware – first-class weapon systems – appropriate to the various domains in which NATO operates, but even more on the people who operate the systems and those who have command and staff responsibilities. The leadership and expertise of each individual, our shared values and common sense of commitment to doing the right thing make the Alliance an extraordinary powerhouse. I am proud to serve with a group of such superb people who constantly seek to improve our decision-making processes, command structure, political and military concepts and warfighting capabilities.

As we seek to modernise NATO from within, we need external perspectives and suggestions for how to improve. We need to be challenged – conceptually and intellectually. We must replace old thinking with new ideas. That is how we thrive and excel. I welcome and encourage an open debate because NATO is not relevant merely to the few; it is important to all who care about peace, security and prosperity. We need critical studies to continue our discourse on how to protect our members' citizens. *Future NATO* is a prime example. I recommend this excellent volume to policy- and decision-makers, military professionals of all ranks and students of statecraft and international relations. I appreciate the comprehensiveness of this paper and its prudent advice.

**General Tod D Wolters**
Supreme Allied Commander Europe
Commander, US European Command

# INTRODUCTION: AN ALLIANCE FOR THE 21ST CENTURY

## JOHN ANDREAS OLSEN

NATO is the most successful political and military alliance in recent history. It remains the single most important contributor to security, stability and peace in Europe and North America. It is vital to the 1 billion Europeans and North Americans who benefit from the political and military framework it provides every day, including over 100 million East Europeans who live in freedom since the fall of the Iron Curtain. The Alliance's inner strength derives from a unity of purpose founded on shared values of democracy, individual liberty, human rights and international law. The muscle behind those values is credible deterrence and collective defence and, importantly, a solemn commitment to Article 5 of the Washington Treaty: an attack against one member is to be considered an attack against all. The Alliance's political decision-making relies on an inclusive process of security and defence consultations, continuous engagement with all members and ultimately the principle of consensus: a democratic norm that gives the Alliance political legitimacy and military credibility. While NATO is designed for US leadership, all constituent members have a voice in shaping NATO decisions. More than seven decades of peace represent a monumental accomplishment; the ability to find strategic cohesion among the members, from the original 12 to the current 29, is extraordinary.[1]

## NATO: Past and Present

NATO has proven such a successful organisation thanks to 'constancy of purpose and strategy-making' in the form of persistent cooperation while

---

[1]  North Macedonia will become NATO's 30th member state as soon as all 29 NATO members have ratified North Macedonia's accession protocol.

simultaneously adapting to the ever-evolving strategic environment.[2] The formal establishment of the Alliance on 4 April 1949 was part of a broader effort to meet three objectives: to deter Soviet expansionism; to prevent the revival of nationalist militarism in Europe through a strong US presence on the continent; and to encourage European political and military integration. These objectives served NATO well throughout the Cold War period.

With the disintegration of the Soviet Union and the dissolution of the Warsaw Pact, the Alliance adapted to new geopolitical circumstances. NATO's partnership programme began with the North Atlantic Cooperation Council (NACC) in 1991 and the Partnership for Peace (PfP) in 1994, under which NATO reached out to the former Warsaw Pact states and Soviet republics to help stabilise their transitions to independence and democracy, prepare them for possible NATO membership in accordance with Article 10 and provide a model for those that could not or would not join for one reason or another.

NATO also reached out to Russia, offering a strategic partnership, and began operations 'out of area' in the Balkans with the objective of enabling a Europe 'whole, free and at peace', a phrase coined by then President George H Bush in 1989.[3] The way in which the Alliance developed after the end of the Cold War demonstrated that it could adapt to strategic circumstances very different from those that prompted its creation in 1949. When Al-Qa'ida attacked the US homeland on 11 September 2001, NATO took the historic decision to invoke Article 5 for the first time. Since then, NATO members and partner countries have fought jointly in Afghanistan to thwart terrorism and extremist violence and to project security.

In February 2014, NATO again witnessed fundamental shifts in the global security setting, but this time closer to home. Russia seized and illegally annexed Crimea, violating Ukraine's territorial sovereignty, the UN Charter, the 1975 Helsinki Accords, the 1994 Budapest Memorandum, and the 1997 NATO–Russia Founding Act. Russia's breach of international law, opposition to Western liberal values and aggressive behaviour in the subsequent years has united all members of the Alliance to take decisive action, as manifested at three successive NATO summits.

NATO's 'strategic reset' began at the Wales Summit in 2014. All NATO members condemned Russian actions and committed themselves to reversing the trend of declining defence budgets. Through the Defence

---

[2] For an excellent overview, see Diego A Ruiz Palmer, 'A Strategic Odyssey: Constancy of Purpose and Strategy-Making in NATO, 1949–2019', *NDC Research Paper Series* (No. 3, June 2019).

[3] US Diplomatic Mission to Germany, 'A Europe Whole and Free', Remarks to the Citizens in Mainz by President George H Bush, 31 May 1989, <http://usa. usembassy.de/etexts/ga6-890531.htm>, accessed 26 January 2020.

Investment Pledge, all European members of the Alliance agreed to spend at least 2% of their gross domestic product (GDP) on defence by 2024, with at least 20% of those funds allocated to development of new capabilities and research programmes. As a result, defence expenditure by countries other than the US has now grown for six consecutive years.

At the 2016 Warsaw Summit, Allies agreed to increase NATO's military presence in the eastern part of the Alliance by deploying four battalions in Estonia, Latvia, Lithuania and Poland on a rotational basis. These defensive multinational battalions, known as the Enhanced Forward Presence (EFP), demonstrated the strength of the transatlantic bond and made clear that an attack on one Ally would be met by forces from across the Alliance. Allies also endorsed a tailored forward presence in NATO's southeastern flank, built around a Romanian framework brigade under Multinational Division Southeast (MND-SE). These forces are still in place, as are air-policing operations along NATO's eastern borders.

At the Brussels Summit in 2018, NATO leaders agreed to a major update of the Alliance's command structure, adding more than 1,200 personnel and two new commands. The Joint Force Command (JFC) in Norfolk, Virginia, is tasked with guaranteeing that sea lines of communication between Europe and North America remain open and secure, ensuring that military forces can move quickly across the Atlantic and within Europe. The Joint Support and Enabling Command (JSEC) in Ulm, Germany, will improve the movement of troops and equipment across borders within Europe. At the summit, leaders also agreed on a NATO Readiness Initiative (NRI), the 'Four Thirties': Allies are committed to having 30 mechanised battalions, 30 air squadrons and 30 combat vessels ready to use within 30 days or less.

The decisions at Wales, Warsaw and Brussels amount to a revitalisation of credible deterrence and collective defence in response to Russia's belligerence. At the same time, NATO has dealt with a series of other issues, including international terrorism, continued operations in Afghanistan and a strengthening of NATO's southern flank. The last few years have also seen updated and improved contingency plans and exercises, including Exercise *Trident Juncture* in October–November 2018. Led by NATO and hosted by Norway, the Alliance's biggest exercise for many years included 250 aircraft, 65 ships and almost 10,000 ground vehicles. It was an exercise in collective defence to test responsiveness and the ability to operate together under harsh conditions. When NATO heads of state and government met in London in December 2019 to celebrate the Alliance's 70 years of existence and mark the 30<sup>th</sup> anniversary of the fall of the Berlin Wall, all leaders confirmed solidarity, unity and cohesion and agreed to continue implementing the decisions from the three previous NATO summits.

This assessment should not lead to the conclusion that NATO can be content with the status quo. NATO at 71 faces a number of complex, severe and ever-evolving challenges that test the Alliance's purpose and unity: some are familiar while others are new; a few are imminent, and many are long-term; some come from within while others are driven by external actors. We are entering a period of phenomenal change.

## Future NATO

It is within this space – between NATO's proud past and the unpredictable and, in many ways, daunting future – that we offer this Whitehall Paper, in which eminent experts explore themes that are central to how NATO must adapt to new realities to stay relevant. The first three chapters examine NATO's enduring relevance, the importance of US leadership and military presence in Europe, and NATO's evolving partnerships. The authors demonstrate that there can be no substitute for NATO, that deterrence defence and dialogue remain the foundation of the Alliance and that various partnerships have always been central to NATO's commitment to peace and security.

The next three chapters focus on external challenges from a geographical perspective. The authors assess the potential threats emanating from Russia and China, respectively, against the backdrop of great power competition, and the issues confronting NATO's southern flank, especially terrorism and irregular migration. A separate chapter is dedicated to NATO's responsibilities in the maritime domain, from the North Atlantic to the Mediterranean and the Black Sea. Collectively, these chapters demonstrate that NATO's future security depends on handling challenges and competition in the military and economic spheres – from Russia in the short term and China in the longer term, thwarting terrorism in its various forms, and maintaining control of the strategic waters that connect NATO members.

Chapters VIII and IX offer responses to current and future challenges. The authors suggest how NATO could handle new technologies and domains in the digital age, sustain and enhance its conventional military capabilities, and manage the ever-present issues associated with arms control and nuclear weapons – both its own and those of potential adversaries. The paper closes with thoughts on operational requirements that will better prepare NATO to execute its missions in the traditional air, sea and land domains in addition to the new warfighting domains of cyber and space.

In sum, this Whitehall Paper offers a series of assessments with functional, institutional and conceptual recommendations on how to ensure that NATO remains credible and capable, united and ready, for the coming decades. Collectively, the authors identify three internal challenges as first order of business: to *re-energise* NATO's cohesion based on democratic values; to *revitalise* US leadership and the transatlantic bond between North America and Europe; and to *rebuild* European defence structures and force posture. Addressing these systematically and comprehensively will in turn enable NATO to meet the three principal external challenges facing it, which can be summarised as *containing* Russia, *comprehending* China and *countering* terrorism. The common denominator for these three challenges from state and non-state actors is that they threaten a rules-based international order with emphasis on Western values – the very foundation of the Alliance.

It is the fundamental belief in a multinational defence organisation dedicated to sustaining peace, stability and security that has ensured a unity of purpose throughout the decades. That cohesion, underpinned by a sense of collective responsibility, has repeatedly overcome internal differences and external pressures. The main conclusion from the authors of this paper is that NATO has remained relevant for more than 70 years because it has stayed committed to the values and principles of the original Washington Treaty, while at the same time adapting as necessary to the changing strategic environment. It is this basic recipe that forms the foundation for future NATO.

# I. NATO's ENDURING RELEVANCE

## SVEIN EFJESTAD AND ROLF TAMNES

The signing of the North Atlantic Treaty in April 1949 represented a true global turning point, as it secured stability in Europe and peace and freedom for those countries that swore the oath of allegiance. More than seven decades later, NATO has come of age. The number of member states has grown steadily from the founding 12 to the present 29.

NATO has faced many serious challenges over the years; in 1953, the US threatened to reconsider its commitment to European security; in 1966, France removed its forces from NATO's integrated military command; more recently, US President Donald Trump has questioned NATO's viability. The future could prove no less complicated. NATO operates in an environment characterised by pervasive instability and long-term strategic competition.

Yet we should not despair. Analysts have long told us that the Alliance is on the verge of crisis and impending collapse. Indeed, among the oldest refrains in the West are that NATO is in crisis, deterrence is breaking down and the Alliance needs new thinking.[1] Such warnings have served as a barrier rather than a pathway to new understanding. The Alliance has hardly faced any existential crises.[2] No countries have seriously considered exercising their rights under Article 13 of the Treaty to terminate membership, additional countries are eager to join and NATO's partnership programmes continue to expand. NATO is still vigorous, remaining the strongest and most enduring military alliance in modern history.

---

[1] Kori Schake, 'NATO's in Crisis! (Again)', *Foreign Policy*, 16 February 2017.
[2] Wallace J Thies, *Why NATO Endures* (New York, NY: Cambridge University Press, 2009), p. ix; Seth A Johnston, *How NATO Adapts: Strategy and Organization in the Atlantic Alliance since 1950* (Baltimore, MD: Johns Hopkins University Press, 2017). See also Sten Rynning, 'NATO's Futures: The Atlantic Alliance Between Power and Purpose', *NDC Research Paper Series* (No. 2, March 2019).

The indispensable leadership of the US is a key reason for the strength and vigour of the Alliance; without the US, no unifying Western military cooperation can exist. Sometimes member states have found it difficult to tolerate admonitions from the US that they should conform to US priorities and simply 'stand up and be counted', but lack of US leadership has been more worrying.

The powerful ties between North America and Europe are another important reason for the success of the Alliance. NATO is a bargain with roots in the hearts and minds of its members.[3] Their commonality of purpose and interest is encapsulated in the 14 articles of the North Atlantic Treaty, which makes strong statements in its few words. The profound message of the Treaty is about togetherness, not threats that must be overcome. A careful study of the Treaty and the history of the Alliance shows that NATO has substantial leeway to adjust to new situations without amending its founding principles.

This chapter focuses on NATO as a stabiliser and a guardian of independence, freedom and the rule of law. It examines the many dilemmas posed by Russia, terrorism and China in particular, underscoring the importance of maintaining US leadership, of revitalising NATO's political functions and consultation, and of finding efficient ways to operate as a military organisation. The chapter highlights four broad recommendations for the future.

## A Community Based on Common Values

The 20th century was the age of extremes, with enormous human losses and suffering in wars, revolutions, political experiments, terror and purges. The horrors of war spurred movements for peace and human rights, reflected in the 1945 UN Charter. Yet by 1949 the Soviet Union and its allies represented not only a military threat, but also a competitive political system – communism – which violated freedom and fundamental rights. The rise of the Soviet Union to become a superpower, its domination of Eastern Europe and its expansionist ideology led to the Cold War and the formation of NATO.

The Alliance born in 1949 is unique for many reasons. At its core, it is a political community based on shared interests and common values, exceptional in history and in the world today. The principles of democracy, individual liberty and the rule of law figure prominently in the preamble to the North Atlantic Treaty. Today, these values are under heavy pressure. Populism and nationalism are on the rise in member

---

[3] Stanley R Sloan, *NATO, the European Union, and the Atlantic Community: The Transatlantic Bargain Challenged* (Oxford: Rowman & Littlefield, 2003), p. 1.

states and placing a strain on the Western community, but so far, checks and balances have contributed to correcting any serious deviations from the fundamental values defined in the Treaty.

While NATO safeguards fundamental principles, not all Allies have always been democracies. Portugal had authoritarian rule until 1974, and Greece and Turkey in particular have, at times, drifted away from democratic principles. NATO will probably have to accommodate such deviations in the future, but that does not mean that membership comes without obligations. The Alliance should make more vigorous use of its various venues and instruments, including the NATO Council, to scrutinise infringements on fundamental rights and abuse of power. That said, organisations such as the Council of Europe and the EU have a more explicit obligation to enforce adherence to democratic values and human rights. Unlike NATO, the EU has procedures to bring its members to court based on charges of undemocratic practices.

## US Leadership and Allied Discord

NATO has been crucial in protecting Western ideological, economic and security interests, and strong US leadership is a prerequisite for NATO to survive and prosper. Although Western Europe 'invited' the US into post-war Europe, the remarkable power of the US defined the objectives and strategy of Atlantic cooperation.[4] Most member states have established bilateral ties with Washington within the Alliance's collective framework. At the heart of the success of US leadership is its arsenal of soft power, which enables the US to influence the preferences of Allies through appeal and attraction rather than coercion. Equally important, the US has the economic and military power to make NATO's security guarantee credible.

While all NATO members agree on the need to retain US leadership in the Alliance, the history of NATO has included various conflicts among Allies. Indeed, some of the transatlantic rifts were deep, but most of them were short-lived and never threatened the existence of the Alliance. NATO, and Western military cooperation more broadly, have natural stamina, which takes the form of strong self-healing tendencies.[5] For example, in 1953, US Secretary of State John Foster Dulles threatened to undertake an 'agonizing reappraisal' of the US commitment to European security if the rearmament of West Germany through the European Defence Community came to nothing. This was soon forgotten when

---

[4] Geir Lundestad, 'Empire by Invitation? The United States and Western Europe, 1945–1952', *Journal of Peace Research* (Vol. 23, No. 3, 1986), pp. 263–77.
[5] Thies, *Why NATO Endures*, pp. 200, 218, 294.

Germany became a NATO member instead. NATO Allies quickly put their differences behind them following the Suez crisis of 1956, which actually stimulated a rapprochement between the UK and US. In 1966, French President Charles de Gaulle put NATO's cohesion to a serious test when he withdrew France from NATO's integrated military structure and expelled Allied troops from France. But NATO decided to avoid a showdown, the political relationship remained strong and the consequences were mostly economic and practical.[6] In the early 1980s, thousands of protesters took to the streets in reaction to NATO's dual-track decision in 1979 to deploy new nuclear weapons in combination with an offer to Moscow to negotiate. The movement was more noisy than politically strong, and NATO's decision reflected a remarkable degree of consensus, with the process serving as a model for future decision-making.[7]

The combination of occasional upheaval and underlying stability also characterises NATO after the Cold War. NATO was successful in adapting its strategy and organisation to deal with new risks and threats, although the process was seldom smooth or swift. The break-up of Yugoslavia presented the first test; in the view of the US, the future of NATO now depended on European military participation 'out of area'. NATO troops fought in the Balkans, culminating in the Kosovo war in 1999, and achieved their primary goals. The war in Iraq, by contrast, was a transatlantic tragedy, and in February 2003 NATO had what then US Ambassador R Nicholas Burns called a 'near-death experience',[8] yet even this crisis did not last long. In Afghanistan, the overall results of an extensive international engagement are discouraging, but NATO countries stood side by side and succeeded in building a coalition of members and partners. Fighting transnational terrorism united NATO, and many European states rallied behind the US intervention to safeguard NATO's continued relevance. Transactional deal-making of this kind has played an important role in shaping NATO policy and preserving the Alliance.[9]

---

[6] Timothy Andrews Sayle, *Enduring Alliance: A History of NATO and the Postwar Global Order* (New York, NY: Cornell University Press, 2019), pp. 34–37, 45–75; Frederic Bozo, *Two Strategies for Europe: De Gaulle, the United States, and the Atlantic Alliance* (Oxford: Rowman & Littlefield, 2001).

[7] Catherine McArdle Kelleher, 'The Present as Prologue: Europe and Theater Nuclear Modernization', *International Security* (Vol. 5, No. 4, Spring 1981), pp. 150–68; Leopoldo Nuti et al. (eds), *The Euromissile Crisis and the End of the Cold War* (Redwood City, CA: Stanford University Press, 2015).

[8] R Nicholas Burns, 'NATO Has Adapted: An Alliance with a New Mission', *New York Times*, 24 May 2003.

[9] For the Norwegian case, see Norwegian Ministry of Foreign Affairs and Ministry of Defence, 'A Good Ally: Norway in Afghanistan 2001–2014', Official Norwegian Reports (NOU 2016: 8), 6 June 2016, <https://www.regjeringen.no/contentassets/

Strong US leadership remains crucial in almost all aspects of NATO decision-making, but it cannot be taken for granted. President Barack Obama's administration played a relatively passive role in NATO during the Libya operation and failed to enforce a 'red line' in Syria. The re-emergence of Russia as a revisionist power has renewed NATO and US engagement in collective defence. While President Donald Trump has criticised most European NATO members in no uncertain terms for not contributing enough, his administration has delivered what the Obama administration promised.[10] NATO has strong support in the US Congress, among the American people and in the military and intelligence communities. Future presidents will most likely recognise the need for NATO and individual Allies to work with the US in coping with challenges posed by major antagonists, but the US demand for greater burden-sharing is reasonable and will not disappear when new leaders take office in Washington.

## Institutions and Consultation

The North Atlantic Treaty makes few references to institutions. Article 9 states: 'The Parties hereby establish a Council, on which each of them shall be represented ... The Council shall set up such subsidiary bodies as may be necessary; in particular it shall establish immediately a defence committee'. Article 4 prescribes consultation whenever the territorial integrity, political independence or security of member states is threatened. Thus consultation, whether among all member states or smaller groups, is at the heart of the Alliance. Such deliberations draw on advice from intelligence organisations and a broad variety of government agencies, and involve large segments of the foreign policy and defence sectors in member countries. Extensive exchange of views contributes to improve cohesion and unity.

Since its founding, NATO as an organisation has grown significantly. It may at times seem overly bureaucratic and slow to act, but compared to many major international organisations NATO has a well-deserved reputation for being able to act rapidly when necessary. Even so, the challenges ahead are so many and complex that the Alliance must revitalise political functions and consultation.

Instead of establishing formalised hierarchies, giving the larger powers an exalted status, NATO's trademark has been institutional

---

09faceca099c4b8bac85ca8495e12d2d/en-gb/pdfs/nou201620160008000engpdfs. pdf>, accessed 5 February 2020.

[10] Frederick Ben Hodges, 'Adapting NATO to Deter Russia: Military Challenges and Policy Recommendations', in Mark Voyger (ed.), *NATO at 70 and the Baltic States: Strengthening the Euro-Atlantic Alliance in an Age of Non-Linear Threats* (Tartu, Estonia: Baltic Defence College, 2019), p. 18.

inclusiveness combined with informal diplomacy in smaller groups. This structure has given smaller states both a security guarantee and the opportunity to take part in formulating common Western policies and initiatives. These benefits are so central to them that they have endured occasional pressure from the most powerful Ally to conform to its views. For the US, NATO offers the best way of influencing developments in Europe. US bases and facilities on European soil can sustain operations in and outside Europe. The Europeans also remain the US's most consistent allies; they contribute more willingly than other countries to international military operations in Africa and Asia and give welcome political legitimacy to operations that are overwhelmingly American in composition and scope.

All member states agree that NATO must have strong military power. Yet that is not enough for the Alliance to endure. In some formative periods, members were concerned that NATO could lose sight of its raison d'être – the broader political perspective and the idea of togetherness – which would require more consultation. On three occasions, NATO asked elder statesmen and prominent diplomats to think beyond the military dimension. In 1956, the 'three wise men' – Lester B Pearson, Gaetano Martino and Halvard Lange – proposed extending political consultation and NATO's role in non-military fields. The 1967 Harmel report introduced the timely dual-track policy comprising both deterrence and détente, and in 2010 the Albright report struck a fine balance between the need to deal with a broader portfolio of tasks after the turn of the century and the need to maintain the core commitment to security. They all contributed to enhancing the legitimacy of NATO.[11]

In the years to come, NATO should expand consultation, both to maintain political unity and to be better prepared to deal with a great number of challenges. A more energetic engagement should address traditional and emerging threats and arms control, as well as violations of fundamental rights within the Alliance. Furthermore, NATO should devote more attention to the security policy consequences of climate and technological change and to the negative security impacts of conflicts over trade and economy.

## Command Structures and Multinational Operations
NATO has been a unique arena for building competence and interoperability – the gold standard for member states and partners. One

---

[11]   For a good overview, see Sten Rynning, 'Sustaining NATO by Consultation: Hard Choices for Europe', *Journal of Transatlantic Studies* (Vol. 17, No. 2, June 2019), pp. 139–56.

of the early tasks of the Alliance was to set up an integrated structure for collective defence operations. In autumn 1950, it made truly revolutionary decisions that paved the way for the establishment of joint headquarters, contingency plans, designated forces and extensive exercises. With the end of the Cold War and NATO's concentration on operations outside its traditional area of responsibility, many elements of this structure were terminated or scaled down. The main purpose of the radically reformed command structure was now to serve expeditionary operations, and by the turn of the 21$^{st}$ century NATO's understanding of what would be required in high-end operations at home had atrophied. From this unpromising starting point, NATO has shown remarkable energy and dynamism in rebuilding collective defence in Europe since 2014.

In a crisis or war, NATO's military response will stand on stronger ground should the Council decide unanimously on a given course of action. However, as pointed out in Article 5, each member has an individual obligation to act and assist. With no consensus in the Council, individual Allies can therefore act immediately. This illustrates the two dimensions of Allied cooperation, encompassing both NATO as a whole and coalitions of the willing.

From the early 1950s, NATO had two supreme commanders: one for Europe (SACEUR) and one for the Atlantic (SACLANT). Each led strong regional headquarters. Plans for reinforcing member states in a conflict traditionally relied on countries with an interest in specific regions, in addition to the major powers that had more resources and wider horizons. In an actual conflict in Europe, the military campaigns would have been executed by coalitions of the willing within NATO's framework. Since 1990, coalitions of the willing have become widespread in Europe and a normal way of organising operations outside the territory of NATO member states. Today, most of the Western military missions in the Middle East and Africa fall into this category. Typically, such operations and activities involve many NATO Allies and partner countries. Such coalitions represent a useful addition to UN operations and engagements led by regional organisations and make important contributions to the security of NATO countries bordering the volatile south.

The EU's contribution to hard security will likely remain modest in the future, notwithstanding occasional rhetoric about the desire to form a strategic alternative to a US-reliant defence organisation. The EU lacks the decision-making apparatus, command arrangements and forces needed to deal with high-intensity operations. Even the most powerful European countries do not have the resources or qualifications to lead a multinational European coalition in such endeavours. Thus, Europe without the US and NATO would be much more vulnerable to intimidation and pressure from authoritarian countries. Yet the EU has important complementary roles to play in stabilising the Eurasian region and in engaging Russia. EU initiatives can also contribute to reinvigorating collective defence in Europe, for instance through the EU's military mobility initiative, launched in 2017, to facilitate cross-border permissions and reduce physical hindrances, enhancing the movement of troops and military equipment throughout Europe.

In addition, bilateral and 'minilateral' defence collaboration has grown significantly, partly outside NATO and the EU. The breadth of this kind of cooperation is illustrated by the Visegrad Group, the Northern Group, the Nordic Defence Cooperation, the Joint Expeditionary Force, the Framework Nation Concept and the European Intervention Initiative.[12] Most of these initiatives and organisations strengthen European security, but there is a fine balance between the gains they may achieve and their potential to create fragmentation and duplication. In the final analysis, NATO still provides the best overarching framework for policy coordination and high-end operations.

## Threats and Challenges

The security challenges confronting Western democracies are increasingly multifaceted and daunting, and NATO will have to deal with many of them. Russia, terrorism and China represent the most immediate and complicated threats. Erosion of democracy and the rise of populism in Europe and in the transatlantic world weaken joint leadership and support for the Alliance. In addition, climate change may cause social and political disruption and lead to unprecedented conflicts and wars. Many new technologies – including quantum computing, artificial intelligence, autonomous systems, long-range hypersonic precision-guided munitions and cyber warfare – may make existing concepts and capabilities obsolete. This would increase the difficulty of defending territories, institutions and citizens, heighten the advantage of taking the offensive and undermine strategic stability.

### Containing Russia

Russia has re-emerged as the most demanding strategic contender to NATO by increasing its military and wider hybrid capabilities and activities and demonstrating its willingness to use them. To understand and manage

---

[12]   Rolf Tamnes and Robin M Allers, 'Just Do It: Bilateral and Minilateral Cooperation to Invigorate European Security', in Robin M Allers, Carlo Masala and Rolf Tamnes (eds), *Common or Divided Security? German and Norwegian Perspectives on Euro-Atlantic Security* (Frankfurt: Peter Lang Publishing Group, 2014).

Russia, NATO must bear in mind how strongly geography and history shape that country's political and strategic culture. George Kennan, founder of the containment strategy, wrote in 1946 that 'at [the] bottom of [the] Kremlin's neurotic view of world affairs is [a] traditional and instinctive Russian sense of insecurity',[13] but he also emphasised that Soviet power was 'highly sensitive to [the] logic of force'. For this reason, the USSR would rapidly withdraw 'when strong resistance is encountered at any point'.[14] These insights should remain NATO's guide to dealing with Russia.[15]

The main objectives of President Vladimir Putin's policy are to secure the survival of his regime, restore influence in essential parts of the former Soviet empire and remake Russia as a $21^{st}$-century great power. Russia has maintained and strengthened its nuclear capabilities across the board, and only NATO and the US's extended deterrence can provide a counterbalance in and for Europe. Russia has also invested heavily in the modernisation of its conventional forces with remarkable, if incomplete, success. Russia's military posture is oriented towards enabling rapid transition from peace to war, seizing the strategic initiative and employing military power to intimidate and coerce adversaries. To achieve this, Russia has optimised its force posture for high readiness, prompt mobilisation and quick movement of large forces over long distances.

From NATO's perspective, two interrelated parts of Russian strategy are particularly worrying. The first is the systematic build-up of anti-access/area-denial (A2/AD) capabilities, from the Arctic to the Mediterranean, relying on steadily growing numbers of air-defence systems and long-range precision strike weapons, many of them both conventional and nuclear capable, as well as cyber and electronic tools to degrade NATO forces. Under this anti-access umbrella, Russia has forces at high readiness close to NATO borders, which could make Russia capable of seizing territory. Thus, in regions adjacent to Russia, the Alliance risks being faced with a fait accompli or with paralysing Russian pressure in a crisis situation. The second cause for concern is Russia's 'bastion' concept to protect its strategic nuclear submarines in the north, which includes sea control of northern waters, sea denial down into the Greenland–Iceland–UK (GIUK) gap, and force projection into the North

---

[13] See George Kennan, 'The Charge in the Soviet Union (Kennan) to the Secretary of State', telegram, National Security Archive, 22 February 1946, <https://nsarchive2.gwu.edu/coldwar/documents/episode-1/kennan.htm>, accessed 5 February 2020.
[14] John Lewis Gaddis, *George F. Kennan: An American Life* (New York, NY: Penguin Press, 2011), pp. 201–22.
[15] For further information about the four pillars of Russian strategic culture, see Stephen R Covington, 'The Culture of Strategic Thought Behind Russia's Modern Approaches to Warfare', Harvard Kennedy School, Belfer Center, October 2016.

Atlantic to disrupt trade flows and military manoeuvre. Russia's bastion defence and anti-access capabilities potentially imperil the link between North America and Europe.

Since 2014, NATO has reinvigorated key elements of deterrence and defence, having spent nearly a quarter of a century focusing on expeditionary warfare. This includes forward presence in the Baltic Sea and Black Sea regions, regional defence plans and a new military strategy tailored to deal with Russia, terrorism and the volatile south. A new maritime posture has created the basis for safeguarding the strategic sea link across the North Atlantic. NATO is improving its command structure, as exemplified by two new commands that address high-end requirements: the Joint Force Command (JFC) in Norfolk, Virginia, tasked with defending the North Atlantic, moving forces and material across the high seas and projecting power; and the Joint Support and Enabling Command in Ulm, in charge of enabling the movement of forces across Europe. These steps would have been impossible without US leadership and resources.

To dissuade Russia, NATO escalation must be as seamless as possible, leaving no room for Russia to carry out a fait accompli assault and decouple the US from Europe. High-quality intelligence and effective decision-making are of critical importance. In a crisis, NATO or key Allies should make a firm decision to engage immediately, forcing Russia to realise that further steps will bring it into war with NATO. This would also require NATO to have both long-range weapons and some reinforcement units in place to respond immediately, and substantial Allied reinforcements must begin to move as well, signalling to Russia that it will face overwhelming superiority.

NATO's most urgent task in a predominantly conventional scenario is to set up credible deterrence and defence in the first critical period in the most exposed areas, particularly in the Arctic, Baltic and Black Sea regions and the East Mediterranean. The Alliance must reinforce its forward presence and strengthen its capacity to degrade Russian anti-access weapons. This is a very difficult undertaking, particularly since Russia continues the build-up of such weapons, but its A2/AD 'bubbles' are not impenetrable.[16]

For NATO to reinforce its northern, eastern and southern flanks, the strategic bridge across the North Atlantic must remain open.[17] Port facilities and underwater infrastructure such as fibre-optic cables require additional protection. NATO must clarify which commands should have

---

[16] Robert Dalsjö, Christofer Berglund and Michael Jonsson, 'Bursting the Bubble: Russian A2/AD in the Baltic Sea Region: Capabilities, Countermeasures, and Implications', FOI-R—4651–SE, March 2019.

[17] The term 'flank' has become commonly used but it is misleading as it implies there is a main direction or front, which is no longer the case in Europe.

the main responsibility for particular regions and tasks. There is every reason, both politically and operationally, to assign the responsibility for the sea bridge and force projection into Europe to the JFC. While the size and quality of US forces are overwhelming, only a minor part of them might be available in Europe in a crisis. This underscores the need for stronger participation by other Allies. One of NATO's key priorities is to regain its advantage in anti-submarine warfare, benefiting from new technologies and non-traditional modes of operation such as unmanned autonomous systems, stealth and endurance, as well as non-acoustic detection and offensive cyber operations.

*Hybrid Threats*

NATO deterrence has been designed for conventional conflicts, and its stronger deterrence and defence posture will make a conventional warfare scenario less likely. However, Russia is also the primary practitioner of hybrid warfare, characterised by the effort to achieve strategic and material ends by fragmenting the Western alliance and vulnerable societies. These types of activities are not unprecedented but cyber capabilities have strengthened the ability to collect intelligence information, attack infrastructure, and manipulate political and public debates. Incremental disruption backed by the threat of using hard power may weaken NATO's decision-making in an actual crisis by breaking political resolve and undermining the ability to employ military power.[18]

In 2014, the Alliance adopted an enhanced NATO cyber defence policy and stated that a cyber attack on a member state could lead to the invocation of Article 5.[19] Yet hybrid actions are often ambiguous and difficult to attribute, making them particularly difficult to deter and counter. Moreover, the primary responsibility for responding to hybrid threats rests with each country, and the tasks are divided between a great number of ministries with different threat perceptions. Domestic politics and legal constraints further limit the ability of democracies to counter largely covert offensive operations.

Good intelligence and early-warning indicators play key roles and may help to establish red lines. The members of the Alliance have

---

[18] Dmitry (Dima) Adamsky, *Cross-Domain Coercion: The Current Russian Art of Strategy*, Proliferation Papers No. 54 (Paris: IFRI, November 2015), p. 10. 'Hybrid' is a useful term to describe what has been written here. It does not mean that hybrid warfare is a formal comprehensive Russian strategic concept, however. See Sandor Fabian, 'The Russian Hybrid Warfare Strategy – Neither Russian Nor Strategy', *Defense and Security Analysis* (Vol. 35, No. 3, 2019), pp. 308–25.

[19] Susan Davis, 'NATO in the Cyber Age: Strengthening Security & Defence, Stabilising Deterrence', NATO Parliamentary Assembly, October 2019.

committed themselves to enhancing their resilience against hybrid techniques, which is an essential aspect of deterrence by denial, and the countries have every reason to strengthen these efforts further. NATO and its members must also build a strong cyber capacity to target adversaries on their territories if necessary. Some member states have offered up the use of their offensive capabilities, and this is a promising beginning.

The need to improve response to complex hybrid threats and assaults provides yet another reason for extensive consultation and coordination in the Alliance. Stronger defence might enable NATO and the EU to deter high-order aggression, but they are unlikely to be able to compel Russia to stop everyday 'grey zone' actions.[20]

### Terrorism and the South

The asymmetric threat posed by terrorism concerns the Alliance as a whole but is most keenly felt by Allies in the south. The Alliance has a joint responsibility for projecting stability, notably by assisting member states under threat and by lending direct support to weak and unstable states in the region. However, NATO is only part of the solution. Most military operations in the region are conducted by coalitions of the willing. They are more flexible and effective than NATO in these efforts. More broadly, the complexities and crises of the south can only be eased or contained if many states and institutions are willing to act together and apply significantly more economic and military resources than today.

### The Rise of China and the Tectonic Shifts in Global Geopolitics

China sees itself as a re-emerging great power, with a rapidly expanding economy and a powerful military. In the long term, it will most likely become a global military actor, with footprints on all continents. NATO must agree on a unified strategy towards China to maintain its relevance and effectiveness.

The rise of China affects NATO countries directly in fields such as the economy, technology and cyber warfare, and indirectly because the US is becoming absorbed in a strategic competition with China. The most urgent security problems are China's aggressive cyber activity and the prospect that Chinese investments in NATO member states' critical infrastructure could undermine the Alliance's military interoperability and

---

[20] Stacie L Pettyjohn and Becca Wasser, 'Competing in the Gray Zone: Russian Tactics and Western Responses', RAND Corporation, 2019; John R Deni, 'The Paradox at the Heart of NATO's Return to Article 5', *RUSI Newsbrief* (Vol. 39, No. 10, November/December 2019).

thus military cooperation. Fifth-generation technology, in which Chinese firms play a leading role, is very important for emerging weapon systems and operational effectiveness. More broadly, Chinese investments and activities in the West may bring Western nations, industries and organisations into a state of deep economic and political dependency that can undermine freedom of choice.

China will therefore be a major issue in the transatlantic conversation. Since many of NATO's member states have common concerns in this regard, it should be possible to make China into a unifying issue. Even smaller countries, which might hesitate to take a strong position because they are particularly vulnerable to Chinese sanctions, may be ready to stand up as participants in actions led by the major Western states. NATO could play a pivotal role by defining its goals and strategy towards China, and by securing the necessary military basis. However, NATO is not intended to address technological and economic challenges; other institutions, such as the EU, are better suited to take on these tasks.

The entente between China and Russia is of concern geopolitically. Their cooperation is enhanced greatly by their shared hostility towards the US and their desire to undermine the leading position of the US and liberal values and institutions. They promote more authoritarian rule in many areas of the world. It would serve Western strategic interests if China and Russia were divided. This is not unlikely in the long term. A steadily more powerful and assertive China could eventually also become a serious challenge to Russia. As part of its competitive strategy, the West and NATO should look for opportunities to foster such a split.

## Recommendations for the Future
### Enhance Dialogue
NATO should expand consultation and coordination, including in the Council, both to maintain political cohesion and to be better prepared to deal with a great number of dangers in the security environment. This effort must address not only traditional military challenges, but also ways to deal with complex hybrid threats. Extensive consultation and unified positions on arms control and confidence-building are also of great importance. Furthermore, the Alliance should have continuing discussions and consultation about the security policy consequences of fundamental shifts such as climate and technological change.

Some non-military issues are key to maintaining unity and legitimacy and must receive more attention. This includes the need for the Alliance to scrutinise more vigorously infringements on fundamental rights and abuses of power, in accordance with the preamble of the Treaty. It also includes the economic dimension. Article 2 of the Treaty points out that member countries should seek to eliminate conflict in their international economic policies and encourage economic collaboration between any or all of them. This guidance has been neglected in NATO consultations for almost 40 years. Today, deep conflicts of interest concerning trade and other economic issues threaten to undermine NATO cohesion, so extensive consultation is essential to forestall negative security policy consequences.

NATO has established formal contacts with a wide web of external partners. In the current uncertain security environment, NATO should expand consultation with like-minded organisations and nations around the world. Such consultation would improve management of economic diversity and conflicts of interest.

Even more important, meaningful dialogue with existing and potential adversaries is crucial to forestall crises and catastrophes. Consultation must devote significant attention to Russia and China. Without dialogue, tensions between the great powers may more easily lead to misunderstandings, inadvertent escalation and conflicts with devastating consequences. New technologies exacerbate this problem. Offensive cyber, anti-satellite and anti-submarine weapons, precision-guided hypersonic missiles, and stealth and unmanned weapons put a premium on the offensive, which in turn will weaken deterrence and stability during crises.

In conjunction with its rearmament, Russia increasingly exhibits disregard for arms control agreements, for instance in its breach of the Intermediate-Range Nuclear Forces (INF) Treaty. To make matters worse, proliferation of sophisticated weapons is a global phenomenon, with China as the key challenge because of its lack of interest in joining substantive arms control negotiations. Even so, NATO should adhere to the dual-track Harmel formula of deterrence and détente or defence and dialogue. NATO should actively seek out opportunities to continue confidence-building discussions and engage in arms control talks.[21]

*Increase Burden-Sharing*

Article 4 on consultation and Article 5 on assistance are the most important elements of the North Atlantic Treaty. Article 3 is also of great value, emphasising not only collective defence but also individual capacity and self-help. This was a crucial part of the bargain in Congress when the US decided to support the idea of a transatlantic alliance: American assistance had to be matched by equivalent European sacrifices.[22] Since the birth of

---

[21] Douglas Lute and R Nicholas Burns, 'NATO at Seventy: An Alliance in Crisis', Harvard Kennedy School, Belfer Center, February 2019.

[22] Lawrence S Kaplan, *The United States and NATO: The Formative Years* (Lexington, KY: University Press of Kentucky, 1984), pp. 75–86.

NATO, politicians and academics alike have repeatedly and vigorously debated how to fairly share the transatlantic burden and how much particular members should contribute to the collective defence provided by the Alliance.[23]

Historically, the US has always covered the overwhelming part of the costs, in the form of weapons assistance, infrastructure means and forces available. It spends 3.4% of GDP on defence; the rest of NATO collectively spends less than 1.6%.[24] Asymmetric defence spending has led to much frustration in the US, with Congress accusing Europeans of free-riding.[25]

NATO has developed criteria to measure member capabilities and contributions to the Alliance. Defence spending in proportion to GDP is an important benchmark. After 2014, it became a central issue as a result of both US pressure and the new threat environment, which prompted recognition that most NATO countries had neglected the capabilities required for high-intensity warfare. The 2014 Wales Summit agreed on the pledge that all members should move towards spending 2% of GDP on defence and dedicate 20% of those expenditures to investments in new capabilities within a decade. The 2% benchmark is important politically, especially because it has become a symbol of commitment to the Alliance as a whole.

President Trump's ambivalence about NATO's value and his insistence that members should keep to this pledge brought the Alliance into a new confrontation. Washington continues to remind Allies that US capabilities and resources are also limited, and that the US will focus increasingly on its costly competition with China. Thus, it is in the interest of the Alliance to share the defence burden more equitably, both to meet US expectations and to build stronger defences after many years of neglect. The effort is already yielding results: defence spending has increased in most European member states.

*Craft Competitive Strategies*
Russia has succeeded in taking advantage of opportunities, particularly by exploiting the vulnerabilities of others. Its military planning reflects a

---

[23] Geir Lundestad, *The United States and Western Europe Since 1945* (Oxford: Oxford University Press, 2003); Wallace J Thies, *Friendly Rivals: Bargaining and Burden-Shifting in NATO* (Armonk, NY: M E Sharpe, 2002).
[24] NATO, 'Defence Expenditure of NATO Countries (2013–2019)', 29 November 2019.
[25] Peter Viggo Jakobsen and Jens Ringsmose, 'Burden-Sharing in NATO: The Trump Effect Won't Last', *NUPI Policy Brief* (No. 16, 2017).

combination of strategic thinking and opportunism. By contrast, NATO's mode of thinking has been static and predictable, ceding the initiative to Russia to decide when, where and how to act. NATO planning is now moving cautiously in the right direction: to alleviate NATO's current fragmentation one overall plan will apply to all domains and regions, which will make it easier for the Alliance to think and act strategically. Yet, while this is promising, NATO must undertake more vigorous measures. NATO should begin by setting its priorities and force goals based on a competitive mindset and a comprehensive net assessment of the key balances of military power and must exploit the relative weaknesses of the potential adversary. Russia targets soft political and physical spots in the West, so the West must develop options to deal with Russia in the same way, focusing on its vulnerabilities and exploiting NATO's advantages and the Western technological edge.[26]

## Expand Regional Approaches

All members must act together to counter the threats facing the Alliance. Stronger regionalisation of core activities is the least expensive way to ensure proper deterrence and defence for all. Most NATO members are small states with limited ability to sustain significant contributions to deployed operations. Hence, they can primarily make a difference in their own region, by employing their national forces and by jointly formulating initiatives tailored to regional needs, thereby also reducing the scope of reinforcement requirements. The substantial differences in the challenges facing the southern, eastern and northern NATO members underscore the value of a regional approach. NATO regionalism also facilitates the engagement of partners in the various regions. Non-aligned countries such as Finland and Sweden have close ties to their NATO neighbours in the north as well as to the US and the UK. Regionalism makes it easier to develop Northern Europe into a functional unity.

Further, a clearer regional approach will improve the functioning of NATO's headquarters. In critical situations, member states may have to transfer command of their forces to NATO headquarters, so they must have full confidence in the competence of the command structure. During the last few decades, personnel from most member countries have participated in almost all headquarters, but today's situation calls for improving regional competence and situational awareness. Double-hatting of commanders and headquarters could link forces and structures from

---

[26] Anthony H Cordesman, '"Burden-Sharing" and the 2% of GDP Solution: A Study in Military Absurdity', CSIS, 23 October 2019; Rolf Tamnes, *The High North: A Call for a Competitive Strategy*, RUSI Whitehall Paper 93 (London: Taylor and Francis, 2018).

many countries in effective ways without creating duplication. Personnel from countries in the region or countries with substantial military activities and commitments in that region should constitute the bulk of the staff, because they have the greatest insight into threats and the best knowledge of the relevant forces and infrastructure. Regional headquarters would also facilitate interaction with the civil societies in the region.

Some fear regionalism, especially because it could lead to fragmentation. Yet fragmentation should rarely occur if regional plans and structures are clearly anchored in the central organisation and the sole supreme commander has the authority to direct operations holistically, which in turn underscores the importance of giving SACEUR extensive authority.

## Conclusion

The idea of togetherness among Allies and the commonality of purpose and interests remain strong. No member states have seriously considered leaving the Alliance and additional nations seek to become members. US leadership is indispensable and continues to play a key role in policy and defence. While the future role of the US has become more unpredictable, we should assume that it will sustain its interest and military footprint in Europe to deal with Russia and terrorism, and to retain Europe as a partner to counter an increasingly powerful China. Indeed, partnership with Europe is indispensable for the US to maintain its central position in international affairs.

NATO is in the process of strengthening its deterrence and defence concept for dealing with conventional conflicts. This stronger deterrence and defence posture will make a conventional warfare scenario less likely. However, as noted above, Russia is also the primary practitioner of hybrid warfare. Responding to grey-zone or hybrid threats and assaults will prove challenging. Better intelligence and early warning will make it easier to identify and clarify the character of the threat. Building more resilient societies and systems, in addition to robust cyber capacities to target adversaries, will contribute to enhancing both deterrence and defence. Overall, NATO should formulate a bolder strategy for countering hybrid attacks by taking advantage of its own strengths and of adversaries' weaknesses. This should be a part of the broader effort to craft competitive strategies in the Alliance, based on a competitive mindset and a comprehensive net assessment of the key balances of military power.

Stronger regionalisation of core activities will enhance efficiency and military strength. NATO should also continue to foster coalitions of the willing in the spirit of allied operations, which make the Alliance particularly robust.

President Trump has broad support in the US for pushing allies in NATO and elsewhere to spend more on defence. It would benefit the Alliance to share the defence burden more equitably, both to accommodate US expectations and to build stronger defences after many years of neglect.

NATO should expand consultation, not only on military threats, but also on violation of fundamental rights, security policy consequences of climate and technological change and the impact of conflicts on trade and economy. The Alliance must extend its dialogue with like-minded organisations and states around the world and keep the door open for adversaries to join discussions. Arms control and confidence-building should have a prominent place on NATO's agenda, with an emphasis on a dual approach involving both deterrence and dialogue. Consultation must also devote significant attention to China.

NATO is a strong war machine, but in these critical times it must expand its perspective and think more boldly to preserve the unity and strength of the Alliance. In some formative periods, NATO initiated studies to identify the prospects of strengthening NATO's political dimension, with findings captured in the 1956 'three wise men' report, the 1967 Harmel report and the 2010 Albright report, respectively. The recommendations of the Stoltenberg report, to be presented at the NATO Summit in 2021, have the potential to re-energise transatlantic cooperation, enabling NATO to continue to flourish in the geopolitical environment of the 21$^{st}$ century.

# II. PERMANENT DETERRENCE AND THE US MILITARY PRESENCE IN EUROPE

## ALEXANDER R VERSHBOW AND PHILIP M BREEDLOVE

The two decades following the end of the Cold War and the collapse of the Soviet Union saw a significant shift in US defence priorities and resources away from Europe and towards other regions. The strategic assumption was that a post-Soviet Russia would be less antagonistic in the European security environment, and would potentially even become a strategic partner. As a result, the US drew down its combat forces in Europe, while European defence spending and readiness declined. Despite signs that Russia had begun pivoting to a more hostile posture towards NATO – with cyber attacks against Estonia in 2007, the invasion of Georgia in 2008 and Russia's subsequent major force build-up and modernisation programme – the US and its NATO Allies failed to fully anticipate and direct resources towards deterring the growing threat. In 2014, when Russian forces invaded Crimea and then eastern Ukraine, they were totally unprepared.

Russia is not the only potential threat to NATO and the rules-based international order. The new security environment is both complex and multifaceted, with growing instability emanating from the Arctic, China, Iran and beyond. China continues to emerge as a great power competitor, while nuclear weapon proliferation to Iran and North Korea, in addition to the developing impacts of climate change, could represent further threats to the US and the transatlantic community. Terrorism and other forms of extremism, in addition to uncontrolled migration and human trafficking, present considerable challenges to the southern flank of Europe. NATO needs to think of defence and security in all domains and with a 360-degree perspective. Member states must share the burden by investing in military capability, contributing forces throughout NATO's 'area of responsibility' and strengthening partnerships beyond the Alliance itself.

As Europe is the US's closest and most important ally, its security is critical to the US global agenda. To both Europe and the US, the transatlantic relationship is more important now than ever. With the wider set of geopolitical challenges in mind, this chapter focuses on the bottom line of the Alliance: its significance for permanent deterrence and defence in North Central Europe. Given Russia's readiness, proximity and ability to quickly mass firepower close to its borders, along with its demonstrated behaviour and objectives in the region, North Central Europe remains arguably the most vulnerable potential flashpoint between Russia and the US and NATO.[1]

## The Russian Challenge

The legitimacy of President Vladimir Putin's regime, which is strained by a stagnant economy and rising popular dissatisfaction but is not likely to fall soon, is underpinned by the narrative of 'encirclement of Russia by a hostile West'. This provides the pretext for Russia to demonstrate its power on the world stage. As a result, Moscow will continue to assert its interests most boldly in its self-declared sphere of influence in Eastern and North Central Europe, and may employ force when it deems that necessary, or when it sees a low-cost opportunity to increase Russia's political or military power. However, Putin will avoid actions he believes would provoke a major military response from the US and NATO, which makes the Alliance's deterrent posture even more crucial. If Putin questions the credibility of NATO's deterrence because of perceived military inadequacy or Alliance disunity, a carefully calculated military incursion into NATO territory is not unimaginable.

A 2018 report by the RAND Corporation found that Russia has built up roughly 80,000 combat personnel in the Western Military District and maintains significantly more tanks, armoured fighting vehicles and heavy artillery in the vicinity of the Baltic states than Allied forces.[2] Given the need for a credible deterrent posture, this current conventional overmatch in North Central Europe, especially in the Baltic states, remains a matter of serious concern for the Alliance.

---

[1] This chapter is adapted from a report published by the Atlantic Council in 2018. For further arguments and references, as well as concrete recommendations for an enhanced US force posture, see Alexander R Vershbow and Philip M Breedlove, 'Permanent Deterrence: Enhancements to the US Military Presence in North Central Europe', Scowcroft Center for Strategy and Security Issue Brief, Atlantic Council, December 2018.

[2] Scott Boston et al., *Assessing the Conventional Force Imbalance in Europe* (Santa Monica, CA: RAND Corporation, 2018), <https://www.rand.org/pubs/research_reports/RR2402.html>, accessed 5 February 2020.

Meanwhile, the Kremlin will seek to exploit the perception that the West is weak and divided by internal disputes and differences between Washington and its European allies. It will continue to increase the intensity, complexity and scope of its disinformation, cyber and other hybrid activities aimed at destabilising Western societies and discrediting democratic values. Russia will also likely continue to ignore its international treaty obligations, seeking to undermine the security architecture set by the US and Europe, and to develop and modernise its capabilities, including the introduction of advanced electronic, cyber and hypersonic technologies.[3] The Kremlin has already demonstrated a new focus on advancing high-precision strike capabilities as part of what it terms 'pre-nuclear deterrence'.

At the same time, Russia is expected to further modernise, if not increase, its nuclear arsenal and to complete the re-nuclearisation of occupied Crimea. Russia's continued ambiguity regarding its doctrine and 'escalate to de-escalate' strategy will force NATO to consider the possibility that the Kremlin will use asymmetric, or even nuclear, capabilities to settle a conventional conflict on its terms. This has significant implications for the US and NATO in terms of force posture and potentially strategy and doctrine. Signs indicate that Russia will sustain its large-scale exercises, particularly the strategic military exercises like *Zapad* 2017, *Vostok* 2018, and *Tsentr* 2019 that rotate yearly between Russia's geographic military districts.[4] Russia's armed forces are likely to increase the complexity of these exercises, maintaining and honing the ability to rapidly mass and deploy conventional forces with little warning. This will enhance Russia's

---

[3] This goes hand in hand with a number of Kremlin decisions to ignore international treaty commitments, including its suspension of the Conventional Armed Forces in Europe Treaty (CFE) in 2007, violations of the Intermediate-Range Nuclear Forces Treaty (INF), circumvention of Vienna Document guidelines on notification and observation of military exercises, and implementation issues and violations of the Open Skies Treaty (OST). See Gustav Gressel, 'Under the Gun: Rearmament for Arms Control in Europe', European Council on Foreign Relations, 28 November 2018, <https://www.ecfr.eu/publications/summary/under_the_gun_rearmament_for_ arms_control_in_europe>, accessed 7 February 2020; Aaron Mehta, 'US, Russia Remain at "Impasse" Over Open Skies Treaty Flights', *Defense News*, 14 September 2018, <https://www.defensenews.com/air/2018/09/14/us-russia-remain-at-impasse-over-nuclear-treaty-flights/>, accessed 7 February 2020; Daniel Boffey, 'NATO Accuses Russia of Blocking Observation of Massive War Game', *The Guardian*, 6 September 2017; Congressional Research Service, 'Russian Compliance with the Intermediate Range Nuclear Forces (INF) Treaty: Background and Issues for Congress', 7 December 2018, <https://fas.org/sgp/crs/nuke/R43832.pdf>, accessed 7 February 2020.
[4] Russian Ministry of Defence, 'Armed Forces Exercises', <https://eng.mil.ru/en/ mission/practice/all.htm>, accessed 25 January 2020.

ability to prepare for and execute potential offensive operations that could overwhelm forces on NATO's borders, increase the chances of Russia using a snap exercise to disguise another illegal intervention abroad (as Russia did in 2014 to hide its mobilisation before the launch of its operation to occupy and annex Crimea), and raise the risks that a miscalculation by a NATO Ally or Russia could escalate to full-scale conflict.[5]

## The US and NATO Response

The US and NATO have taken several significant steps to respond to multiple aspects of the Russian challenge, and made some notable progress in the political, economic and other non-military spheres since 2014. The US spearheaded sanctions, some in tandem with EU partners, to punish Russia for its illegal annexation of Crimea, hybrid war and aggression in eastern Ukraine, cyber attacks on critical infrastructure in Estonia and Ukraine, and interference in US and European elections. The US, with the support of Congress, also established the Global Engagement Center (GEC) at the Department of State to counter Russian disinformation and influence operations in Europe and Eurasia. NATO has created its own hybrid analysis branch focused largely on Russia, signed a watershed joint declaration to boost NATO-EU cooperation against hybrid threats in 2018 and, alongside the EU, supported the establishment in Helsinki of a multinational European Centre of Excellence (COE) for Countering Hybrid Threats in 2016. Many European Allies have also honed their approaches for holistically countering Russian malign influence. The Baltic states, for instance, routinely publicise reports on Russian interference and subversive efforts in their countries while also making efforts to reduce their dependence on energy imports from Russia.[6] On the military front, the US and its NATO Allies have made important strides by adapting their force posture to better cope with Russian conventional and hybrid threats.

### *NATO Force Posture in Europe Post-2014*

The Alliance's initial response to the invasion of Ukraine consisted of 'assurance measures' focused on air defence and surveillance, maritime deployments and military exercises. At the Wales Summit in September

---

[5] Johan Norberg, 'The Use of Russia's Military in the Crimean Crisis', Carnegie Endowment for International Peace, 13 March 2014, <https://carnegieendowment. org/2014/03/13/use-of-russia-s-military-in-crimean-crisis-pub-54949>, accessed 7 February 2020.

[6] Raphael Cohen and Andrew Radin, 'Russia's Hostile Measures in Europe,' RAND Corporation, 2019.

2014, Alliance leaders promulgated a Readiness Action Plan designed to combine some of these short-term assurance measures with 'adaptive measures' that offered a longer-term response to Russian aggression. NATO's fundamental deterrence strategy, implemented through the Wales Summit initiatives, relied heavily on relatively small spearhead units such as the Very High Readiness Joint Task Force (VJTF). While these initiatives improved NATO's capacity to reinforce its eastern flank in a crisis, many Allies and NATO leaders argued that a more significant military response was required. They called for a more robust and multinational forward presence backed up by swift reinforcements to signal to Russia that the cost of breaching NATO borders would be too high.[7]

Following decisions taken at the July 2016 Warsaw Summit, the Alliance took that next step by deploying its Enhanced Forward Presence (EFP) battlegroups – ground combat forces – to Eastern and North Central Europe. These battalion-sized EFP deployments added an element of 'deterrence by tripwire' to NATO's Readiness Action Plan, making clear to Russia that any aggression would be met immediately – not just by local forces, but by forces from across the Alliance.

While EFP marked a major increase in Allied force presence, the combination of these forward-deployed elements and host-nation forces still faced significantly larger, and more heavily armoured, combined Russian forces immediately across the border. Thus, defending North Central Europe in a crisis would still require substantial reinforcements from Western Europe or the US. Mobilising and deploying these forces would take time, giving Russia a window for opportunistic aggression that could result in a fait accompli and require the Alliance to undertake costly offensive action to regain the territory seized.

At its July 2018 Brussels Summit, NATO sought to shorten this time–distance gap. The NATO Readiness Initiative (NRI) – the so-called 'Four Thirties' plan – requires 30 ground battalions, 30 air squadrons and 30 major naval combat vessels to be ready to deploy and to engage an adversary within 30 days. NATO also undertook significant command structure reform to help address this problem and ensure the structure was fit for purpose in today's security environment. Allied leaders agreed to establish the Joint Support and Enabling Command (JSEC) in Germany to facilitate the support and rapid movement of troops and equipment across Europe, and a Joint Force Command (JFC) in Norfolk, Virginia, to protect crucial sea lines of communication and transport between North

---

[7] Alexander Vershbow, 'A Strong NATO for a New Strategic Reality', keynote address at the Foundation Institute for Strategic Studies, Krakow, 4 March 2016, <https://www.nato.int/cps/en/natohq/opinions_128809.htm>, accessed 7 February 2020.

America and Europe. In a related effort, NATO and the EU have collaborated on a 'military mobility' initiative, under Dutch leadership, which seeks to facilitate the rapid movement of forces and equipment across the European continent, especially as it relates to border crossings, infrastructure requirements and legal regulations. In light of increasingly aggressive cyber incidents perpetrated by Russia, during the Brussels Summit in 2018 NATO also established a Cyberspace Operations Centre – staffed by experts with access to military intelligence and real-time information on threats in cyberspace – to coordinate NATO's and member states' cyber deterrent capabilities and possible offensive cyber operations in a crisis.

These decisions from the Wales, Warsaw and Brussels Summits have accumulated and evolved, laying the groundwork for deterrence by rapid reinforcement: the Alliance's current strategy for defending its eastern frontier.


*US Force Posture in Europe Post-2014*
The drawdown of US troop levels in Europe since the end of the Cold War had long raised concerns among commanders at US European Command (USEUCOM) and in the Office of the Secretary of Defense.[8] However, it was not until the events of 2014 that those concerns were shared widely by the White House and the Pentagon.[9] In conjunction with NATO's Readiness Action Plan, the US reacted quickly to reassure Eastern and Central European allies of its dedication to the Alliance's collective defence mission.

Immediately after Russian troops entered Crimea, USEUCOM deployed company-level elements from army units based in Europe to Estonia, Latvia, Lithuania and Poland as a reassurance measure. The US also recognised a need for deterrence in the air domain, deploying six F-15s to the Baltic Air Policing mission, along with an aviation detachment of 12 F-16s to Łask, Poland. This tripwire force, similar in doctrine to NATO's subsequent EFP deployments, allowed the US to immediately reinforce the defence and deterrence mission while it slowly expanded deployments and funding.

Many of these efforts were supported by the FY2015 European Reassurance Initiative (ERI), which in 2017 became the European Deterrence Initiative (EDI) and has continued to expand under President

---

[8] Kathleen H Hicks et al., *Evaluating Future US Army Force Posture in Europe: Phase II Report* (Washington, DC: Center for Strategic and International Studies, June 2016), p. 15.
[9] Philip M Breedlove, 'Statement of General Philip M. Breedlove', Senate Armed Services Committee, 30 April 2015.

Donald Trump's administration, providing significant funding to support US presence, exercises and training, enhanced prepositioning and improved infrastructure throughout Europe.[10] Under the auspices of the ERI, the US slowly augmented its presence, particularly in North Central Europe. By 2016, the US had added roughly 4,000 rotational troops to Europe, in addition to the brigade combat teams (BCTs) already permanently deployed to Europe. In Grafenwöhr, the US also maintains its largest European training facility, which improves US and NATO force qualifications. Acknowledging that current US and Allied forces in North Central Europe were insufficient for deterrence purposes, in 2017 the US also began nine-month continuous rotations of armoured BCTs to Europe. These continue today in Poland, with detachments deploying regularly throughout Central Europe, and now include periods during which US forces are systematically postured closer to the front line of a potential conflict in North Central Europe to further reduce the time–distance gap and enhance deterrence in the region.

While certainly nowhere near its Cold War level, the US posture in Europe is markedly different today than it was five years ago. The US Army in Europe (USAREUR) currently maintains 35,000 US soldiers in theatre, with 22,000 permanently assigned to USAREUR.[11] The US Army also employs 12,500 local nationals, 11,000 civilian officials from the US Department of the Army and Regionally Allocated Forces rotating through as part of Operation *Atlantic Resolve* – the name given to efforts in response to Russia's actions in Ukraine.[12] In 2018, USAREUR participated in 52 exercises to enhance readiness and interoperability of these forces, involving approximately 29,000 US personnel and more than 68,000 participants from 45 countries.[13] In addition to its major Army units, USEUCOM has at its disposal a number of other land, air and naval assets in its area of operations, totalling more than 60,000 military and civilian personnel.[14]

One major result of the FY2018 EDI was the pre-positioning of US Air Force equipment and airfield infrastructure improvements to support current operations, exercises and activities, and to enable a rapid response to

---

[10] US Department of Defense, 'European Deterrence Initiative: Department of Defense Budget Fiscal Year 2019', February 2018, <https://comptroller.defense.gov/Portals/45/Documents/defbudget/fy2019/fy2019_EDI_JBook.pdf>, accessed 7 February 2020.

[11] Alexander R Vershbow and Philip M Breedlove, *Permanent Deterrence: Enhancements to the US Military Presence in North Central Europe* (Washington, DC: Scowcroft Center for Strategy and Security, Atlantic Council 2019), p. 26.

[12] *Ibid.*

[13] US Army Europe Public Affairs Office, 'Fact Sheet: U.S. Army Europe', 14 November 2018.

[14] Vershbow and Breedlove, *Permanent Deterrence*, p. 27.

contingencies. The FY2019 budget builds on this, funding the European Contingency Air Operations Set deployable airbase system through which equipment is pre-positioned at various locations throughout Europe, which in turn provides a basis for adaptive basing of air forces as an important element of NATO's reinforcement strategy.

## Looking to the Future

The US and NATO have taken significant steps to respond to Russia's actions by first implementing a 'deterrence by tripwire' strategy and then a 'deterrence by rapid reinforcement' strategy. Still, the evolution and implementation of these responses have been incremental, temporary and reactive. Most important, the forces deployed under these strategies have not sufficiently addressed Russia's current advantages in time, space and mass. Given the enduring nature of the Russian challenge, the US and its NATO Allies must implement a more strategic and long-term approach for dealing with Russia, using the full range of political, economic, military and other responses.

### *The Need for an Enhanced Force Posture*

The conventional military pillar of this approach remains fundamental to deterring Russia. The US and the rest of NATO face a pressing need to strengthen their deterrence and defence posture, given the vulnerability of North Central Europe. NATO's current posture relies on the certainty that the Alliance would respond to any aggression quickly, and that all Allies would respond quickly and forcefully to an armed attack. However, that current deterrence posture may still lack sufficient credibility.

Overall, Russia's military forces would be at a distinct disadvantage in a protracted conflict with the US and NATO. In the long term, with the requisite political will, the US and NATO could leverage their advantages in military and economic power to prevail. Nevertheless, the reality remains that Russia's force posture in North Central Europe gives Russia a short-term advantage locally. A determined Russian conventional attack, especially if mounted with little warning, could still defeat current forward-deployed NATO forces in a relatively short period of time. For example, the often-cited 'nightmare scenario' of a limited Russian land grab in the Baltic states could take place well before US and Allied reinforcements from Germany, the rest of Western Europe or the continental US could be brought to bear. Such a fait accompli could paralyse NATO decision-making and ultimately break the Alliance's will and determination to live up to its Article 5 commitments. While the Baltic states present a different context from Russia's last land grab in Crimea, and the likelihood of a Russian incursion into NATO territory is low, the US and NATO must be prepared for any contingency. They can only do this through advance planning and preparation, including the deployment of the proper force mix in North Central Europe. A first step must be to identify and rectify current gaps in the Alliance's force posture in North Central Europe.

*Gaps in US and Allied Force Posture*

First, the Alliance faces readiness challenges that inhibit its ability to get forces to North Central Europe in time to mitigate opportunistic Russian aggression. In some cases, the national forces that would serve as reinforcements as part of the NATO Response Force (NRF) are neither sufficiently ready nor clearly designated. While NATO has made great strides toward improving readiness, command and control, notification mechanisms and targeted exercise regimes – including through linking the NRF and the 'Four Thirties' Readiness Initiative – it must further reduce the time–distance gap.

Second, even after the NRI has been implemented, there could be a gap of up to 30 days between an initial Russian short-warning attack and the arrival of major reinforcements. Closing this gap would rely heavily on airpower to prevent or slow advances by enemy ground forces until NATO reinforcements could reach the front line. A major challenge for US and Allied air forces would be Russia's anti-access/area-denial (A2/AD) capabilities in the region, particularly in Kaliningrad, which allow Russia to create a denied environment that covers significant parts of Poland and the Baltic Sea region. Although not impossible, using airpower to penetrate the A2/AD cover and reinforce the Baltics would increase the risk of escalating the crisis. Russia's mobile S-400 anti-aircraft units would delay US and Allied forces seeking to disable Russian air defences, making it more difficult for NATO to hold the line from the air until reinforcements could arrive. Defeating Russian air defences may also require attacking targets inside Russian territory (such as Kaliningrad), which could risk a retaliatory attack on the US and its NATO Allies, potentially escalating to a nuclear confrontation.

Third, military mobility infrastructure in Europe has deteriorated since the Cold War. NATO's inattention to this issue means that its newer members now lack standardised or uniform infrastructure, while individual Allies have not modernised infrastructure to support large-scale reinforcements to the east. Thus, it remains difficult to move forces and equipment across the continent to the front line in North Central Europe. In addition to border-crossing delays and legal issues, NATO confronts challenges with mapping routes and ensuring there are standardised bridges, roads and rails that can support the transport of troops and heavy equipment. Once in the target region, larger and more advanced reception facilities, training ranges and other logistical requirements are required to enable ingress, egress and warfighting by US and Allied forces. The FY2019 EDI seeks to support some of this development with pre-positioned equipment, improved infrastructure of airfields and other facilities, and additional storage sites for ammunition and bulk fuel. While the establishment of the JSEC and the NATO–EU military mobility initiative are positive steps towards addressing these issues, full implementation will take years. In any case, NATO would need to protect this critical infrastructure from electronic warfare and cyber attacks, in addition to medium-range missile strikes, by Russia.

Fourth, the NATO EFP battlegroups and the US rotational BCT in Poland lack the enablers necessary to ensure mission accomplishment, including early warning and intelligence, surveillance and reconnaissance (ISR) assets; air and missile defence; and long-range fires to create the counter-fire capability needed for a foreseeable contingency. The Baltic states also lack critical front-line requirements, particularly ammunition, anti-tank weapons, short- and medium-range air defence and long-range artillery. The naval component of US and NATO presence in the region could also be increased to protect freedom of navigation, strengthen maritime domain awareness, counter Russian A2/AD capabilities and assist in closing potential gaps in air and missile defences.

Fifth, while notable progress has been made towards developing coordinated battle plans and clear rules of engagement for NATO forces in North Central Europe, the Alliance must also make several political decisions. One key issue will be identifying and agreeing on key indicators and thresholds that would authorise military commanders to begin mobilising, and then deploying, assets and forces. These actions would also require clearly articulated authorities delegated to SACEUR to execute, and perhaps streamline, these actions. A related issue is intelligence-sharing, which helps lay the groundwork for leaders to act. While the Alliance is making strides towards enhancing intelligence-sharing and decision-making processes, more work must be done to help prepare the Alliance to respond to emerging crises in a timely manner.

All these factors inhibit the Alliance's ability to effectively carry out its agreed strategy of deterrence by rapid reinforcement in North Central Europe. They underscore the need to rethink how US forces are deployed to the region, particularly because these forces constitute the most capable part of the Alliance and the US flag sends the strongest deterrent message in NATO's front line region.

## US Political, Diplomatic and Military Considerations

All NATO members have begun to recognise that the Alliance could further improve its deterrence posture, especially in North Central Europe. NATO can, and should, take additional steps to reduce the 30-day readiness gap and enhance its capacity to deter, defend and, if necessary, retake Alliance territory. Given the US role in the Alliance, a significant part of this response will rely on US force posture. While the US has the right to bilaterally negotiate its force posture agreements with potential host nations, any decision about an enhanced US presence in the region would have serious implications for neighbouring states and for the Alliance as a whole. It is in the US national interest to make these decisions in a way that bolsters, rather than diminishes, NATO cohesion. As a result, the US must take a range of political, diplomatic and military considerations into account when deciding how to adapt its force posture in Europe.

A primary issue is how to address competing demands on limited US resources. Prior to the 2018 Brussels Summit, Bulgaria, the Czech Republic, Estonia, Hungary, Latvia, Lithuania, Poland, Romania and Slovakia all urged NATO to discuss an increased military presence in their region.[15] The Baltic states and Poland, in particular, have called for US boots on the ground, ideally permanently, to actively deter Russia, in addition to critical air and naval units to reinforce the limited NATO EFP battalions already in their countries. In 2018, Norway and the US agreed to double the rotational presence of US Marines in the country and deploy them closer to the border with Russia, extending the current six-month renewable rotation periods to five years. Romania and Bulgaria have also recently requested additional US presence.[16]

The US must balance these competing demands and strategically deploy its limited resources. As described above, the current and anticipated threat environment suggests North Central Europe as a priority; however, adapting the US posture in Europe involves defending all of Europe while preserving US capacity to defend its interests globally. Any deployments of additional US forces or capabilities to the region would have to allow Washington to maintain maximum flexibility for their use, while taking into account both political signals and military needs.

*Force Location*
One significant question is whether Poland should be the central host-nation of an enhanced US presence designed to strengthen NATO's eastern flank. Some argue that US forces should be postured forward, in the Baltic states, to deter Moscow from aggression on NATO's eastern frontier. This view is

---

[15] *Radio Free Europe/Radio Liberty*, 'NATO's Eastern Flank Seeks Increased Alliance Presence in Region', 8 June 2018.
[16] Ryan Browne, 'US to Double Number of Marines in Norway Amid Russia Tensions', *CNN*, 12 June 2018.

based on the premise that the Kremlin would not engage in an attack on or so close to US forces, as it would provoke a swift and decisive US response. However, such a posture would mean a shift away from the current NATO strategy of deterrence by rapid reinforcement towards forward defence and could create divisions within the Alliance. Furthermore, the Baltic states lack not only the geographic space needed to help minimise the vulnerability of deployed forces to Russian strikes, but also the required infrastructure to support such an enhanced presence. Building sufficient infrastructure in the Baltics would take a great amount of time and resources, and space remains limited.

Still, modest rotations of US troops to the Baltic states on a regular basis (for example, quarterly) would send an important political signal to enhance deterrence in this critical region. This would be much more feasible if the US were to deploy additional forces in Europe to support rotations that, in practice, demand triple the forces: one unit preparing for the rotation; one executing the rotation; and one transitioning away from the rotation. Rotational forces would also help to avoid reallocation of currently deployed forces from Germany or other Allies, which could have negative political and military consequences for the transatlantic partnership amid already tenuous dynamics.

Further enhancements to the US force posture in Germany would offer many advantages. Existing infrastructure and logistical capabilities could easily support additional forces or assets and make operations and activities cost-effective. Moreover, an enhanced posture in Germany is far less likely to be perceived as strictly focused on Russia. In some ways, this would reduce the risk of escalating tensions with Russia, while preserving US flexibility to deploy the forces elsewhere (for example, to the Black Sea or the Middle East) without undercutting deterrence in Europe's northeast. However, while forces in Germany would be less vulnerable to Russian attack, they would also be further from the front line.

Poland provides an attractive venue for US efforts for a variety of reasons. First, its size and geographic location make it a key staging area for most NATO efforts to defend the three Baltic Allies. Poland already hosts a US presence and maintains some useful infrastructure, reception facilities, training ranges and pre-positioned equipment that could support an enhanced US force posture. The country is also physically large enough to accommodate more forces and is poised to do so through EDI and the additional $2 billion offered by Poland in 2018 to support an expanded US presence.[17] Geographically, Poland provides a way for the

---

[17] In April 2018, Poland submitted to the US a proposal to host, on a permanent basis, a US military division on Polish territory, and offered $2 billion to finance

US to reduce the critical time–distance reinforcement gap without being so far forward that assets and equipment may be considered overly vulnerable, especially given Russia's A2/AD capabilities in the region. Poland's location could also facilitate more frequent and visible rotations to the Baltic states.

Nevertheless, any enhancements to the US force posture in Poland should come with clear additional expectations of the host nation. In addition to investing in infrastructure and upgrading its facilities to meet US standards, Poland should use any augmented US presence as an opportunity to make greater contributions to security and stability in the region. Actions could include deepening and encouraging more cooperation with other Allies and partners, including the Nordic and Baltic states and Germany – perhaps through rotational deployments of German ground and air forces to Polish bases. The Polish government should also emphasise the value of a strengthened US force posture as a political and military deterrent covering all of Europe, stressing that an enhanced US presence symbolises the values and principles for which NATO and the EU stand.

*Permanent vs Rotational Presence*

The US must also consider the level of forces that should be deployed to Europe, and whether those forces should be permanent or rotational. While the initial Polish request for a division-level presence was overambitious both politically and in terms of force availability, another armoured BCT in Europe would significantly enhance the US and NATO force posture in North Central Europe. These forces, along with sufficient key enablers, would strengthen rapid-reinforcement capabilities and enhance deterrence-building activities throughout the wider region. Contributions from individual Allies, whether in the form of troops or enabling elements, would help to fulfil this requirement and increase burden-sharing while simultaneously boosting deterrence by demonstrating Alliance solidarity.

Increasing rotational forces, as opposed to permanently stationed forces, would maintain the current US emphasis on rotational deployments as a way to visibly deter Russia and reassure Allies, while preserving more flexibility for the US to carry out its commitments in the broader region and globally. This would also be consistent with the US concept of 'dynamic force employment' as outlined in the 2018 National Defense Strategy, which seeks to provide 'proactive and scalable options for priority missions' and 'use ready forces to shape proactively the

---

infrastructure for that deployment. See Alan Cowell, 'Fort Trump? Poland Makes a Play for a U.S. Military Base', *New York Times*, 18 September 2018.

strategic environment while maintaining readiness to respond to contingencies and ensure long-term warfighting readiness'.[18] The infrastructure and enabling elements required to support additional rotational forces would convey serious assurance of the US commitment to collective defence in the region. That commitment is further underscored by the many US efforts that have been, and will be, undertaken in North Central Europe through the EDI, especially in Poland, to support deterrence and defence in the region. Deploying these additional forces rotationally would also more firmly support the current NATO consensus on the framework of deterrence by rapid reinforcement.

Rotational units offer other advantages. Such units tend to be more cost-effective and sustainable than large-scale permanently based forces. Rotational forces also usually arrive with higher readiness levels. Their high operational tempo enables them to undertake quick and decisive action and to maintain their heightened level of readiness throughout their deployments. Rotating these units from the US also allows the forces to become familiar with the conditions in more than one place, which can be beneficial, especially given Russia's hybrid activities throughout the region.

*The 1997 NATO–Russia Founding Act*

The scale and location of forces must take into account larger, fundamental concerns stemming from debates within the Alliance over the NATO-Russia Founding Act. In 1997, seeking to reassure Russia that NATO enlargement would not pose a military threat, NATO agreed that 'in the current and foreseeable security environment, the Alliance will carry out its collective defence and other missions by ensuring the necessary interoperability, integration, and capability for reinforcement rather than by additional permanent stationing of substantial combat forces'.[19] Allies have deployed EFP battlegroups and other enhancements to NATO's deterrence posture on the understanding that 'additional permanent stationing' of forces up to the level of a brigade per country is consistent with any reasonable definition of the limits implied by 'substantial combat forces'. Permanently stationing a whole division or brigade in Poland, beyond the EFP battlegroups and other US capabilities already in that country, could cause division among Allies, thereby undermining deterrence. Such a move could

---

[18] US Department of Defense, 'Summary of the 2018 National Defense Strategy of the United States of America: Sharpening the American Military's Competitive Edge', 2018, pp. 4, 7.
[19] NATO, 'Founding Act on Mutual Relations, Cooperation and Security Between NATO and the Russian Federation Signed in Paris, France', May 1997, <https://www.nato.int/cps/en/natohq/official_texts_25468.htm>, accessed 18 January 2020.

also provoke a Russian overreaction; Moscow has hinted it may try to build a military base in Belarus in response to a potential US base in Poland.

Broadly speaking, it is in the US national interest to ensure its deployments remain within the broad Allied consensus on this issue. If, however, Russia were to increase its threat to the Baltic states and Poland, the US and NATO should be prepared to move beyond the Founding Act, whose limits were based on the 'current and foreseeable security environment' when the document was signed.

## Conclusion: Principles for Enhanced Deterrence

Russia currently represents the most serious threat to the West since the end of the Cold War, putting at risk the collective peace and security that the US and its Allies have fought so hard to rebuild and preserve. The Russian challenge, both in Europe and elsewhere, is only one aspect of the current and anticipated security environment, but it is the most significant and pressing one. The US National Defense Strategy underscores this with its focus on great power competition and Russia, providing the strategic impetus and basis for action. The US and its NATO Allies must bolster deterrence and defence against Russia, particularly in North Central Europe, where the Alliance is most vulnerable.

When considering how to enhance the current deployment of US military forces into North Central Europe, Washington should be guided by the following nine principles. Any additional deployment should:

- Enhance the US and NATO deterrent posture for the broader region – not just for the nation hosting the US deployment – to strengthen readiness and capacity for reinforcement.
- Reinforce NATO cohesion.
- Promote stability with respect to Russian military deployments to avoid an action–reaction cycle.
- Be consistent with the US National Defense Strategy and its concept of dynamic force employment.
- Include increased naval and air deployments in the region, alongside additional ground forces and enablers.
- Promote training and operational readiness of US deployed forces and interoperability with host nation and other allied forces.
- Ensure maximum operational flexibility to transfer deployed US forces to other regions of the Alliance or locations throughout the world as necessary.
- Expand opportunities for burden-sharing by NATO Allies, including multilateral deployments in the region and beyond.
- Ensure adequate host-nation support for US deployments.

In addition, the US and NATO should make decisions in a way that strengthens the foundation of shared values and interests on which the Alliance rests (see Chapter I for more on this).

Measures consistent with these principles could build on the existing US presence in Poland and strengthen deterrence for the wider region by increasing the US naval presence, re-establishing a continuous rotational US presence in the Baltic states and promoting greater burden-sharing among Allies. While adding important military capabilities and increasing NATO's capacity for rapid reinforcement, the scale of any enhanced US capabilities should remain within the NATO consensus, thereby ensuring continued NATO cohesion and solidarity.

# III. NATO AS A PARTNER

## MALCOLM CHALMERS

NATO's partnerships have always been central to its relevance and strength. In some cases, these partnerships have taken an institutional form, for example through the 74 cooperative initiatives currently underway between NATO and the EU.[1] But NATO partnership has a broader meaning. From its founding in 1949, NATO has been part of a wider set of Western institutions designed to work together to create a framework for international cooperation after the catastrophe of the Second World War. These institutions have played a key role in ensuring that NATO has become an enduring alliance, unlike the temporary military alliances of the past.

NATO's longevity has resulted not only from its members' need to confront a clear common threat, but also from a strong sense of political community and the wider shared interest that emerged concurrently, generated not only by the Soviet threat but also by a broader set of shared democratic values. NATO's survival rests on the endurance of this sense of community among states that see themselves as 'Western'. If 'the West' were to become an obsolete concept (splintering, for example, along national or continental lines), it is difficult to see NATO's core commitments surviving for long. Broader partnerships, therefore, are the foundation of NATO's continuing relevance.

---

[1] European Union External Action, 'EU-NATO Cooperation: Factsheets', 11 June 2019, <https://eeas.europa.eu/headquarters/headquarters-homepage_en/28286/EU-NATO%20cooperation%20-%20Factsheets>, accessed 26 January 2020. See also EU and NATO, 'Fourth Progress Report on the Implementation of the Common Set of Proposals Endorsed by NATO and EU Councils on 6 December 2016 and 5 December 2017', 17 June 2019, <https://www.nato.int/nato_static_fl2014/assets/pdf/pdf_2019_06/190617-4th-Joint-progress-report-EU-NATO-eng.pdf>, accessed 18 January 2020.

## The Western Ecosystem

The immediate origins of NATO lie in the wartime alliance between the US and the British Empire and Commonwealth, forged in successive summits between President Franklin D Roosevelt and Prime Minister Winston Churchill. The integrated command structure that oversaw the Normandy landings in 1944, and the subsequent Allied victory over Nazi Germany, became the progenitor and model for the integrated command structure that NATO adopted after 1952 and which remains in place today. The special military relationship between the US and the UK continues to be a key pillar of the Western security system, supporting and reinforcing cooperation at an Alliance-wide level. Other nations that provided important contributions to the war effort, including those represented at the time by President Charles de Gaulle's French government-in-exile and volunteer personnel from Poland and other occupied countries, also trace their initial involvement in the Western defence alliance to this period.

This wartime alliance also helps explain the genesis of NATO's current security relationships with Canada, Australia and New Zealand. All three states made important contributions to the war effort, sending large numbers of forces and considerable financial assistance to the UK during its struggle against the Nazis. After the war, Canada became a founding member of NATO, and to this day continues to deploy significant forces for the defence of Europe. All three countries are also members of the Five Eyes intelligence-sharing relationship, which remains a key element of the wider Western security system, helping to build common understanding of the security landscape and, until now, largely impervious to political perturbations.

Over time, the Western organisational ecosystem evolved to include the OECD (founded in 1961) and the G7 (founded in 1976). Both represent important mechanisms for Western countries seeking to develop common approaches and resolve their differences. Despite having different mandates and varying membership, all the organisations mentioned provide opportunities, and indeed obligations, for leaders and senior officials to meet on a regular basis. Therefore, when difficult issues arise, they can be addressed as part of an intense and regular interaction based on strong shared values and perceived interests. This wider network of political, economic and developmental cooperation reinforces the credibility of NATO's security commitments.

## The EU and NATO

The EU has a key place in the Western ecosystem, providing – alongside NATO – one of the two main pillars of institutionalised cooperation on the continent. While NATO's mandate relates primarily to military cooperation and establishes the political framework necessary to the collective use of force, the EU has a much wider mandate. Moreover, while NATO decision-making is entirely intergovernmental, most of the EU's current activities are governed by community-wide institutions, including the European Commission, European Court of Justice and European Parliament, and as a result sovereignty is shared to an extent unthinkable in NATO.

Even though they are governed in very different ways, the EU and NATO each remain key to the success of the other. In the immediate aftermath of the Second World War, US support for European integration was central to the eventual creation of the European Economic Community in 1957, and US support for the role of the EU provided an important source of strength in subsequent decades. The existence of a credible US security guarantee to Europe, underpinned by large forward-deployed forces, allowed European reconstruction and integration to proceed without reopening the dangerous fractures of the past. From a US point of view, its post-war leadership of NATO cemented its position as the world's leading military, as well as economic, power. Crucially, it also helped ensure the broad support of Europe – which even now continues to be one of the world's three largest centres of economic power – for its broad foreign policy priorities.

The synergy between NATO and the European Community once more became evident in their common response to the collapse of the Warsaw Pact after 1989. The newly liberated states of Central and Eastern Europe, followed by the new states emerging from the breakup of Yugoslavia, were united in their shared determination to become part of 'the West' – an aspiration focused primarily on membership of NATO and the EU. This process of enlargement has, in turn, transformed both institutions.

Together, NATO's 14 post-communist members (including North Macedonia) still only account for some 2.9% of total Alliance defence spending.[2] Yet their concerns are now as central to NATO's overall strategy as those of any other member, and they have succeeded in shifting the Alliance's centre of gravity to a considerable extent since they became members. This remarkable enlargement of the West's common security community has been reinforced by the simultaneous expansion of the EU, which now includes 11 of the 14 new NATO member states,

---

[2] Malcolm Chalmers, 'The 2% Target: Spending Increases and the Russian Threat', *RUSI Newsbrief* (Vol. 39, No. 10, November 2019).

with active efforts being made to recruit the remaining three (Albania, Montenegro and North Macedonia) into the EU.

*Joint NATO–EU Initiatives*

Twenty-two members of NATO are also members of the EU, and in recent years the two organisations have been able to develop many joint programmes and actions. Differences over the status of Cyprus between Turkey and other NATO member states still create some obstacles. Despite this, as a result of agreements reached in December 2016 and December 2017, the two organisations have agreed to 74 common initiatives, all of them designed to respond to shared challenges from both east and south.[3] These have included work in areas as diverse as cyber security, maritime security, logistical support for military reinforcements and methods for countering hybrid threats through resilience. In July 2018, the two organisations went further, agreeing an agenda for further shared action in relation to military mobility, counterterrorism and greater resilience against chemical, biological, radiological and nuclear (CBRN) threats.[4]

Effective management of all the areas and activities requires the combined application of both military and non-military aspects of state capability. For example, while NATO militaries are key to combating potential terrorist threats to Europe that develop and mutate in the Sahel or Syria, these forces need to work closely with police and judicial systems throughout the EU. Timely reinforcement of exposed Allies in Eastern Europe during a crisis will depend on the ability to ensure that bridges and roads can carry heavy military traffic, and that border legislation is appropriate for this purpose. NATO's military and intelligence services must collaborate closely with private companies and financial regulators to help ensure that member states can provide effective responses to evolving cyber threats.

## Looking Forward: Partnership Challenges

No human institution is guaranteed to last forever, and international institutions – especially in a world where nationalism is on the ascent – may be particularly

---

[3] EU and NATO, 'Fourth Progress Report on the Implementation of the Common Set of Proposals Endorsed by NATO and EU Councils on 6 December 2016 and 5 December 2017'.

[4] European Council, 'Joint Declaration on EU-NATO Cooperation', July 2018, <https://www.consilium.europa.eu/en/press/press-releases/2018/07/10/eu-nato-joint-declaration/>, accessed 18 January 2020.

vulnerable in this regard. If NATO is to retain its central importance to the security interests of its member states, it must continue to adapt. In the context of this chapter's focus on partnerships, this will require the Alliance to successfully navigate three key challenges: first, development of the EU as a defence and security actor, including ways to address the issues posed by Brexit; second, possible future enlargement of NATO's membership, including partnership relations with neighbouring states that may have a prospect of membership; and third, partnership with countries for which NATO membership is not a prospect, including Europe's neighbour Russia, the Middle East and Africa, as well as more distant countries.

*Partnership and the EU*
The development of NATO has always been closely linked to discussions on whether, and in what form, European defence integration might take place through other mechanisms. The 1948 Western Union Treaty between the UK, France and the Benelux countries was the immediate precursor to the North Atlantic Treaty and, in the absence of US commitment to European security, would likely have become the foundation of new collective security arrangements on the continent. The establishment of NATO's integrated military command structure in 1952 largely subsumed this initiative, with the commander of the Western Union Defence Organisation, Field Marshal Bernard Montgomery, being appointed Deputy Supreme Allied Commander Europe (SACEUR) in April 1951. Subsequently, the French parliament's failure to ratify the treaty establishing the European Defence Community in 1954 paved the way for West Germany to join NATO, and for NATO to take on the primary role in collective military security in Europe.

As the role of the EU has developed since the 1950s, its role in non-military areas of security has expanded substantially. Its current configuration is based on the 2009 Treaty of Lisbon, which established the position of High Representative, supported by an External Action Service, working alongside the Council of Foreign Ministers across the whole range of security and foreign policy issues. In addition, the EU's importance as a single economic and regulatory actor means that it has a central role in the orchestration of many non-military security tools, such as sanctions, development aid, cyber regulation and international diplomacy.

In addition, and of particular relevance to NATO, the EU has sought to develop a Common Security and Defence Policy (CSDP), which commits its members to the 'progressive framing' of a common defence policy, leading to a common defence if and when member states decide that a situation requires action.

Progress towards strong EU-organised defence capabilities has been uneven. In relation to the organisation of EU military missions under a CSDP framework, the EU has launched some important operations in areas where it believed that NATO action was not appropriate. Today, the EU is conducting two military CSDP operations: the European Union Force (EUFOR) mission in Bosnia and Herzegovina (some 600 strong) and the EU anti-piracy naval force off the coast of Somalia (Operation *Atalanta*), along with military training missions in Mali and Somalia. The willingness to conduct future operations through this framework may increase now that the UK has left the EU. As of now, however, most EU member states are only likely to turn to the CSDP as an instrument for collective military action in circumstances where NATO is not available or appropriate.

The EU's role in relation to the provision of defence capabilities is set to become much more substantial. The Permanent Structured Cooperation on Defence and Security (PESCO) mechanism, established in December 2017, has now authorised 47 projects in total, including 'development of a modular and flexible multi-mission European Patrol Corvette; airborne electronic attack for manned and unmanned aircraft; an advanced command, control and communications service architecture for unmanned anti-submarine systems; space-based early warning systems and endo-atmospheric interceptors to detect, track and counter aerial threats including missiles; and a system to insert drones into the Single European Sky system'.[5] The level of EU-funded defence investment will likely increase. Between 2021 and 2027, under current plans, the EU has earmarked €20 billion for defence. This includes €13 billion for the European Defence Fund (EDF), which will finance collaborative research projects involving EU members as well as contribute to weapons development programmes. A further €10 billion for a 'peace fund', designed to pay for equipment (including weapons), has been proposed for support of partner states, including in the Sahel.[6]

These investments are part of a wider trend towards expanding European defence capabilities that can, in turn, contribute to NATO capabilities. Albeit starting from a low base, European states are now beginning to increase their share of NATO defence spending, with NATO

---

[5] European Council, 'Defence Cooperation: Council Launches 13 New PESCO Projects', 12 November 2019, <https://www.consilium.europa.eu/en/press/press-releases/2019/11/12/defence-cooperation-council-launches-13-new-pesco-projects/>, accessed 18 January 2020.
[6] Fergus Kelly, 'EU Launches 13 New PESCO Defense Cooperation Projects', *Defense Post*, 12 November 2019, <https://thedefensepost.com/2019/11/12/new-pesco-projects-eu-defense-cooperation/>, accessed 18 January 2020.

European defence spending growing 18.5% since 2014, while US spending increased by a more modest 4%.[7] Yet it remains to be seen whether PESCO and the EDF are able to deliver effective military capabilities for their member states in the long term. There is concern, both in the US and in the UK, that the exclusion of non-EU contractors from participation in these programmes could further fragment NATO defence markets and perhaps contribute to wider tension between the US and the EU. In practice, given current levels of reliance on US defence technology, and the many examples of close defence collaboration with UK-based suppliers, a significant number of major European defence projects may stay out of the EDF framework to allow the participation of US and British suppliers.

Even as NATO's partnership with the EU becomes more important than ever, it will be complicated by the UK's departure from the EU. Until now, almost all democratic European states were members of the EU, aspired to join in the near future or, in the cases of Norway and Switzerland, engaged in close cooperative relationships with the EU. This will no longer be the case. Although the precise form of the UK's future relationship with the EU is unlikely to be known for some time, the policies of the Conservative majority government, elected on 12 December 2019, point to a Canada-style trade deal with little, if any, formal political or security relationship. Current modalities for cooperation on foreign policy, access to shared police and justice databases, shared development funds and defence industrial cooperation will all come to an end when the transition period expires (currently set for the end of 2020).

Yet the very weight of the UK as a defence and security actor – with the largest defence and development budgets in European NATO, an active global diplomatic network, a seat on the UN Security Council and an activist strategic culture – means that it is bound to become an important pole of influence in debates on the future of European security. It remains to be seen whether this influence undermines EU or NATO cohesion. NATO could play an important role in helping to ensure that the UK and the EU do not drift apart in their approaches to defence and foreign policy now that the UK is outside the EU. But the risk does exist, and it will present one of the key challenges for NATO and the EU over the next few years.

The future of NATO–EU relations, and the related issue of building a new relationship between the EU and the UK, are themselves closely related to NATO's biggest current challenge: President Donald Trump. Three full years in office have not tempered his instincts or preferences in any way. He is still viscerally opposed to European multilateralism, regarding the

---

[7] Chalmers, 'The 2% Target'.

EU as an adversary of the US and viewing the NATO Alliance in primarily transactional terms. NATO is far from being 'brain dead', despite President Emmanuel Macron's claim in the run-up to the 2019 London Summit,[8] but the crisis created by Trump does pose an existential threat to NATO of a type not seen since the Alliance's formation. It is true that, at an operational level, the US remains as engaged as ever, and has been playing a leading part in the reinforcement of the Alliance's eastward defences since 2014. But the heart of NATO is not hardware. It is the sense of being a shared security community, and the shared belief – among potential adversaries as well as member state governments and publics – that the Alliance's security commitments are genuine.

*Partnership and Enlargement*
Since the end of the Cold War, the question of enlargement has never been far from the surface of NATO politics. The decision to accept former Warsaw Pact members into the Alliance helped ensure that no security vacuum emerged in Eastern Europe after Russian military withdrawal from the region, and – alongside EU enlargement – has paved the way towards a wide-ranging modernisation and democratisation of these societies. Yet it also proved to be a central driver for the deterioration of relations with Russia. The turning point came in 1999, a year that saw both NATO's acceptance of Poland, Hungary and the Czech Republic as full members and NATO's decision, despite fierce Russian opposition, to launch military operations against Serbia in response to events in Kosovo. The subsequent enlargement in 2004, in addition to completing the process of incorporating former Warsaw Pact allies into NATO, added three former Soviet republics – Estonia, Latvia and Lithuania – to the Alliance, bringing NATO's eastern frontier to within 100 miles of St Petersburg. Relations with Russia further worsened due to the 2003 invasion of Iraq by the US and other leading NATO states.

It is not possible to judge whether NATO's relations with Russia would have deteriorated even if enlargement had not taken place. What is clear is that the combined effect of NATO and EU enlargement fundamentally changed the geopolitical alignment of the states of Central and Eastern Europe, transforming them into full members of the Western community of like-minded states. The West had expanded, and NATO played a key role in this process.

Enlargement remains a live issue for NATO in relation to three sets of existing Alliance partners. First, and most difficult, is the continuing

---

[8] *The Economist*, 'Emmanuel Macron Warns Europe: NATO is Becoming Brain-Dead', 7 November 2019.

possibility of including other former Soviet republics. Active discussion of NATO membership for Georgia and Ukraine has been a backdrop for relations between these two states and NATO – and also for their relations with Russia – since they became independent countries in 1991. NATO has strong capacity-building and military assistance relationships with both states, with frequent high-level engagements emphasising their importance to the Alliance. Yet these two countries have also been at the heart of the two most serious crises between NATO and Russia in the post-Cold War period: the short Georgian War of 2008 and the Ukraine crisis triggered by the Russian annexation of Crimea in 2014. In both cases, Russia has sought to make it more difficult for NATO to enlarge by creating unrecognised mini-states within the territory of these former Soviet republics, and it is using the same tactic in Moldova, which might also seek NATO membership. Unless and until the countries in question have full authority over their own territories, it is hard to see how NATO can accept them as full members. Yet the launching and prolongation of these semi-frozen conflicts has also served as a powerful driver for pro-NATO sentiment in both Georgia and Ukraine. As a result, NATO policy often appears conflicted in relation to these states – providing military assistance, but carefully calibrated so as not to give the impression of a security guarantee, and holding out the long-term prospect of membership while avoiding signals that might suggest that membership could be granted any time soon.

Second, NATO enlargement in southeastern Europe has not finished. The recent inclusion of Montenegro and North Macedonia, following Slovenia (which joined in 2004) and Croatia and Albania (2009), has left only three states outside the Alliance: Bosnia and Herzegovina, Kosovo and Serbia. The membership prospects for all three depend on, but could potentially contribute to, a lasting resolution of the disputes left over from the Balkan wars of the 1990s. All three are already important NATO partners, and the prospect of membership in both the EU and NATO continues to be a central element in their relations with the rest of Europe. But strong anti-NATO sentiment persists in both Serbia and the Serbian Republic within Bosnia and Herzegovina. The influence of Russia in the region, especially with Belgrade, also plays a key role.

Third, NATO has strong and deepening security partnerships with Finland and Sweden, whose military importance to the Alliance has increased sharply as it shifts focus to its exposed member states in the Baltic Sea region. NATO's ability to reinforce through, and operate from, Sweden and Finland could be key in future contingencies (hybrid or conventional) in this region. Sweden and Finland, for their part, would hope to be able to call on assistance from NATO states should they come under threat. Neither country seems likely to apply for full NATO membership in the near future. In formal terms, therefore, neither could automatically count on an Article 5 guarantee. In other regards, however, both states are full members of the Western security community, importantly including the EU. By emphasising and deepening their military cooperation with NATO and its key members, both states seek to contribute to deterrence of aggression against them. By investing heavily in national resilience, they make clear – to potential adversaries and allies alike – that they take national defence and security seriously. If Finland and Sweden decided to submit applications for NATO membership in the future, there is little doubt that they would be quickly accepted. But existing cooperation arrangements already provide most of the benefits of NATO membership, and the status quo therefore seems likely to remain unless and until some new crisis precipitates a change of heart.

*Wider Partnerships*
In addition to the European countries discussed above, NATO has institutionalised partnerships with other OSCE member states (through the Euro-Atlantic Partnership Council, EAPC, and the NATO–Russia Council, NRC), the seven members of the misnamed Mediterranean Dialogue (MD; Algeria, Egypt, Israel, Jordan, Mauritania, Morocco and Tunisia), the Istanbul Cooperation Initiative (ICI) with some of the smaller states of the Gulf Cooperation Council (GCC; Bahrain, Kuwait, Qatar and the UAE) and a range of individual partners across the globe. The latter include the US's main allies in the Indo-Pacific region (Australia, Republic of Korea, Japan and New Zealand); countries where ongoing and sustained NATO operations take place (Afghanistan and Iraq); as well as Colombia, Mongolia and Pakistan. Some of these countries have contributed forces to NATO operations in Afghanistan and elsewhere; others benefit from personnel exchanges and capacity building. In the case of the NRC, the partnership is designed to be a mechanism for dialogue with a potential adversary.

These partnerships can play a useful symbolic role in demonstrating the ongoing interest of the Alliance in the countries and regions in question, as well as complementing the strong bilateral relationships which NATO member states sustain in many cases. They are particularly valuable where they are part of a wider relationship, based on shared interests, for example in facilitating cooperation with US Asia-Pacific allies in responding to the rise of Chinese power. They are less important where they work in isolation from other regional organisations, involve a highly heterogeneous group of countries within a single process, and/or where significant differences in perspective and interests exist between NATO and the partner countries. This is the case with both the main partnerships with NATO's southern neighbours, the MD and the ICI.[9] As the opening of the new NATO–Istanbul Cooperation Initiative Regional Centre in Kuwait in 2017 suggests, however, these mechanisms continue to develop institutionally.

Taken as a whole, the relatively modest scale of these 'out-of-area' partnerships reinforces the reality that NATO remains at its heart a Euro-Atlantic, and not a global, alliance. In the era of expeditionary operations, when NATO organised major deployments to both Afghanistan and Libya, these global partnerships had an enhanced role. As NATO returns to a more intense focus on collective security, guarding Europe's eastern and southern flanks, the relevance of these wider partnerships has changed again.

## Conclusion: Caring for Partnerships

The success and longevity of the Western alliance, which came into existence only after the Second World War, was made possible by the ability of its leading members to create an institutional architecture that encouraged a sense of a shared future and common interests. NATO, and the security guarantees at its heart, have been a necessary part of the Western enterprise. But NATO has never been enough by itself. If the West is to survive as a coherent entity – and it remains in the interests of its members that it does – then NATO's partnership with the EU will be critical. This is not because institutional arrangements are themselves critical; for all their merit, the 74 NATO–EU agreements are not the primary glue for cross-organisational harmony. Rather, the continuing cohesion of the European security community depends on the recognition by its member states that their security interests can best be pursued through cooperation, that both NATO and the EU have a role to play in supporting those interests and that any friction between them remains relatively insignificant. These conditions are still fulfilled today, but they will require constant cultivation in the years ahead.

NATO's continuing relevance depends on the perception that NATO membership matters, and in particular on the unique nature of its mutual guarantee of security assistance in the event of a threat to any member. As non-members, none of NATO's partner states are formally subject to the benefits (and responsibilities) which membership brings. But this does not mean that NATO has no security responsibility to these states, or vice

---

[9]   Rachid El Houdaigui, 'NATO's Mediterranean Dialogue: What are New Possible Approaches?', Policy Center for the New South, Policy Brief, 7 June 2016, <https://www.policycenter.ma/publications/natos-mediterranean-dialogue-what-are-new-possible-approaches>, accessed 18 January 2020.

versa. Non-members seek partnership with NATO in order to access security capacity-building assistance and improve the chances of NATO assistance in a future crisis. But the extent and scope of these relationships varies considerably between partners and over time. At one end of the spectrum, NATO relationships with Sweden, Finland, Australia, New Zealand and (to a large extent) Japan are rooted in wider shared membership in Western institutions, bilateral US alliance commitments, a strong sense of two-way responsibility and shared democratic values. At the other end of the spectrum, relations with various Middle Eastern states (through the MD and ICI) are less deeply rooted and should be seen primarily as mechanisms for facilitating basic levels of dialogue and security training. Relationships with other European states – Ukraine, Georgia, Kosovo, Serbia and Bosnia and Herzegovina – fall between these two poles, shaped both by a realistic prospect of future NATO membership and by Russia's continuing ability to deploy its power (including through sponsorship of breakaway mini-states) to frustrate such a scenario. In a world of intensifying competition between major powers, NATO's partnership relationships are likely to remain one of the primary fields in which this competition takes place.

# IV. THE EVOLUTION OF THE RUSSIAN THREAT TO NATO

ANDREA KENDALL-TAYLOR AND
JEFFREY EDMONDS

Russia is once again NATO's most significant external challenge. The situation today stands in stark contrast to the almost two decades following the dissolution of the Warsaw Pact and the Soviet Union, when Russia posed little threat to NATO. Absent a clear military threat, NATO struggled to define its relevance and increasingly turned its focus on out-of-area stability operations. Vladimir Putin's return to the presidency in 2012, however, triggered a shift in Russian foreign policy, with the Kremlin growing more assertive internationally. Moscow's illegal annexation of Crimea and subsequent occupation of eastern Ukraine in 2014 hardened US and European perceptions of Russia as a threat, and refocused NATO on countering and deterring Russian aggression.

Since 2014, the Alliance has taken a number of prudent steps to bolster deterrence, including efforts to reinvigorate NATO's culture of readiness (as has been explored in earlier chapters). But to remain effective, NATO must adapt and respond to Russia's evolving foreign policy. This chapter argues that although the broad contours of Russia's foreign policy and views of NATO are longstanding, foreign policy under Putin has evolved in ways that create new challenges for the Alliance. In particular, Putin has placed greater emphasis on countering what he views as US unilateralism and an international order that seeks to marginalise Russia. He has grown more reliant on military means – including cyber tools – to advance his objectives, and more assertive in his efforts to undermine Western democracies and the cohesion among them.

This evolution of Russian foreign policy has implications for the way that Russia approaches NATO. In its attempts to alter the international order and reassert its great power status, Russia has become more brazen in its efforts to undermine NATO cohesion. Russia has relied, in particular, on the increasing use of information warfare and cyber operations that are designed to avoid the risks and costs associated with direct military confrontation with the US and NATO. The growing prevalence of these tactics creates challenges that NATO must address to remain effective. At the same time, however, NATO must not lose sight of conventional Russian threats. Russian hybrid tactics are effective only because they are backed by credible military power. NATO must therefore address both Russian hybrid actions that threaten NATO cohesion and the credibility of Article 5, while also strengthening its military capabilities to better deter Russia from launching any future conflict.

## The Evolution of Russian Foreign Policy

The broad and longstanding contours of Russian foreign policy stem from the Kremlin's primary objective of maintaining the sovereignty of the state and the stability of the regime. Putin believes that only a Russia that is strong at home can be strong abroad, and vice versa, and that the strength of the state derives in part from its stability and unity of purpose. To support such unity, Putin and the Russian government have established a narrative that continually highlights enemies, whether they be domestic 'traitors' or external actors, such as the US. For example, Putin uses the Kremlin's propaganda machine to reinforce the narrative of a Russia under siege from the US and the West. According to this narrative, the West is intent on keeping Russia weak and destabilising the Putin regime through so-called 'colour revolutions' and efforts to promote democracy throughout the world. These narratives are not just for domestic consumption. Putin and the Russian leadership appear to believe that the US seeks to topple regimes that Washington views as unfriendly and to undermine Putin himself. Russia's strategic attitude towards NATO and the West, therefore, is in many ways defensive – as it has been since the end of the Cold War – and is fed by a deep sense of insecurity and distrust of Western intentions.

This longstanding sense of insecurity has led Russian officials to assert Russia's right to maintain nominally independent but compliant states along its periphery – what Russia views as its 'privileged sphere of influence'.[1] For centuries, Russian regimes have had to defend a vast, sparsely settled,

---

[1]   Russian leaders have consistently articulated a policy of maintaining close links with and influence within Russia's neighbouring area. In addition to 'sphere of influence', other terms that Russians use, including 'near abroad' or *Russkiy Mir* (Russian world), illustrate Russian thinking about its relations with neighbouring states. See, for example, Olga Oliker et al., *Russian Foreign Policy: Sources and Implications* (Santa Monica, CA: RAND Corporation, 2009).

multi-ethnic country that lacks significant physical barriers and that borders powerful states and unstable territories. Russia has dealt with this predicament in part by creating buffer zones on its borders that would give its leaders space and time to mobilise the state in the event of conflict. In more recent times, NATO expansion decreased most of the buffer zone that Soviet Moscow enjoyed throughout the Cold War, leading the Kremlin to view NATO's push to the east as a core threat to Russian security. Moreover, that expansion raised the prospect that Russia would lose influence over Georgia and Ukraine – two neighbours that the Kremlin views as critical to its security and wellbeing. Russia views Georgia and especially Ukraine as important to maintaining Moscow's prestige, and because of Russia's history, economic interests and fundamental security concerns. Moscow fears that should it lose influence in these countries, Ukraine and Georgia could develop into strong, prosperous and democratic countries – models of success that would raise Russians' expectations about what is possible and expose the Putin regime to domestic criticism.

In addition to maintaining influence along its periphery and halting NATO's eastward expansion, Russian foreign policy has long focused on reasserting Russia's status as a great power. Russians have historically seen their country as a great nation and its precipitous domestic decline and global retreat in the 1990s created widespread domestic resentment. The Kremlin seeks to be treated as an equal of the US and to ensure that Moscow's interests are taken into account in all major international decisions. Re-establishing Russia's global prestige has been an important source of Putin's domestic popularity. Russia's illegal annexation of Crimea and to a lesser extent its intervention in Syria, as well as Russia's expanded influence in the Middle East and other global hotspots such as Afghanistan, North Korea and Libya have also boosted Putin's domestic standing. However, as public dissatisfaction over Russia's economic stagnation has grown, the popular euphoria over Ukraine and Putin's international accomplishments has waned. Putin's public approval rating stood at 68% in December 2019, down from a high of 87% in August 2014 in the aftermath of Russia's illegal annexation of Crimea.[2]

In addition to these long-term objectives of the Russian state, Putin has emphasised several other, related priorities that have caused Russian foreign policy to evolve over the 20 years he has been in power.[3]

First, Putin has placed great emphasis on countering what he views as US and Western unilateralism. Russian foreign policy has long sought to

---

[2]  Levada-Center, <http://www.levada.ru/en/>, accessed 29 January 2020.
[3]  Brian D Taylor, *The Code of Putinism* (New York, NY: Oxford University Press, 2018).

create a multipolar – or what Russian foreign policy circles describe as 'polycentric' – world where Russia serves as an independent and unaligned pole. Although Russian officials likely understand that Moscow's ability to project positive influence that would attract other countries into its sphere of influence or to shape the policies of other states has declined, Russia seeks to ensure that no other power can dictate terms to Moscow. Putin also appears to view it as his personal mission to oppose what he sees as Western hypocrisy – namely, attempts by the West to uphold international rules and norms when they serve Western interests, and to circumvent those same rules when they impede Western goals. Several leaders, including Turkish President Recep Tayyip Erdogan and Hungarian Prime Minister Viktor Orban, appear to admire and at times emulate Putin's willingness to stand up to the West.

Similarly, Putin has actively focused on countering 'colour revolutions', or what he sees as US and Western efforts to unseat unfriendly regimes by fomenting internal instability. Putin appears to genuinely believe that the US and the West seek to overthrow him and bring about regime change, and he views efforts to promote democracy – especially US efforts – as thinly veiled attempts to undermine his legitimacy. Putin has long sought to counter these initiatives, and his efforts to do so have grown in scope and intensity. Since 2014, Russia has no longer been content to push back against democracy promotion but has actively taken the fight to Western democracies. Because Moscow gauges its power in relation to the US, the Kremlin views weakening these countries as a means of enhancing its own standing.[4] In the NATO context, this means that the Kremlin has accelerated efforts to exploit the fault lines within and between European states and between the US and Europe, and to fuel doubts among vulnerable NATO members about their Allies' commitment to collective defence.[5]

Putin has also increased the emphasis on militarism and grown more reliant on military tools to advance Russian interests. His interventions in Georgia, Ukraine and Syria have reinforced his confidence that military action serves as an effective means of achieving his foreign policy objectives. Putin has seen that the use of military force enhances Russia's bargaining position with the West, and in particular that these types of actions are the most effective way to gain the attention of the West.[6]

---

[4]  Andrea Kendall-Taylor and David Shullman, 'How Russia and China Undermine Democracy', *Foreign Affairs*, 2 October 2018.
[5]  Thomas Graham, 'Let Russia Be Russia: The Case for a More Pragmatic Approach to Moscow', *Foreign Affairs* (November/December 2019).
[6]  Samuel Charap, 'Russia's Use of Military Force as a Foreign Policy Tool: Is There a Logic?', PONARS Eurasia Policy Memo No. 443, October 2016.

Moreover, Russia has modernised its military over the past decade, successfully creating a highly capable force.[7] In this respect, military instruments – including cyber weapons – have become relatively more effective than Russia's soft power or economic tools, suggesting that the Kremlin will continue to rely on military options.

Putin has undertaken more active and assertive efforts to advance Russian objectives. Moscow's increasingly assertive foreign policy is a reflection not of the country's growing strength, but of the perception that US and Western disarray has created an opening for Russia to exploit.[8] In other words, Moscow assesses that the current US-led world order is coming to an end and that rising powers such as China and Russia should have a greater influence in world affairs. Notably, Putin has found common cause with China's President Xi Jinping, and the two countries have deepened cooperation across key dimensions of their relationship, including in the political, economic and defence realms. Despite the historic mistrust and growing power asymmetry between Russia and China, there is potential for Moscow and Beijing to cooperate in the next 10 to 15 years in ways that could threaten US and European interests. Russia and China share an interest in reducing US global influence and undermining the strength and cohesion of US–Europe relations.

Given the growing instability in the international system and the longstanding challenges within the Russian Federation, such as its weak economic foundation, Putin appears to be calculating that he must act now to influence the international order while he still has the ability to do so. The West's failure to mount sufficient opposition to his moves so far, along with challenges internal to the West – such as Brexit, the Yellow Vest protest movement in France and the rise of far-right populist leaders in Europe – have only reinforced his perception that this is a promising path to restoring Russian influence.

## The Evolution of the Russian Military Threat to NATO

The above changes in the emphasis of Putin's foreign policy create challenges for NATO. In particular, Russia has grown far more assertive in its efforts to undermine the political cohesion of NATO member states and complicate

---

[7] Michael Kofman, 'From Hammer to Rapier: Russian Military Transformation in Perspective', Russia Brief 1, University of Oxford, Changing Character of War Centre, January 2018, <http://www.ccw.ox.ac.uk/russia-brief-issue-i>, accessed 7 February 2020; Susanne Oxenstierna and Fredrik Westerlund (eds), 'Russian Military Capability in a Ten-Year Perspective – 2019', Swedish Defense Research Agency, December 2019, <https://www.foi.se/rest-api/report/FOI-R–4758–SE>, accessed 7 February 2020.
[8] Graham, 'Let Russia Be Russia'.

the consensus on which NATO depends. However, it is important to emphasise that although Russia has grown more assertive in its approach to the West, the Kremlin does not seek direct military confrontation with NATO. The Kremlin likely assesses that NATO and the US would be able to eventually achieve a superior correlation of forces near Russia's borders such that Moscow would likely lose a prolonged conventional war.[9] Instead, Russia is pursuing an approach designed to contest the perceived US-led international order – including what the Russian leadership sees as an increasingly aggressive NATO – while avoiding the risks and costs associated with direct military confrontation. Russia therefore has increased its reliance on approaches and tools, often referred to as hybrid war or political warfare, that are designed to undermine NATO while not rising to the level of inciting a military response from NATO.

Central to Russia's more assertive approach to NATO is the Kremlin's increased emphasis on information warfare. The Russian leadership has come to see the information domain as one of the fundamental arenas in which states compete,[10] and therefore attempts to exert influence within this domain to change the political dynamics in countries whose policies are contrary to Russian interests. These efforts are often structured to achieve specific political goals, such as the influence campaigns during the US and French presidential elections in 2016 and 2017, respectively, but can also seek to foster general discord within the Alliance.

The Russian security community has a broad understanding of information warfare that can roughly be divided between technical and psychological aspects.[11] The technological aspect comprises cyber operations, electronic warfare and activities to protect or damage any data- or information-driven assets or activities that can be subject to interruption or destruction. The psychological aspect includes actions during peacetime to shape the attitudes and policy preferences of an adversary's political, military and civilian populations.

Putin's increasingly assertive foreign policy stance is mirrored in its security policies where Russia has deployed its military capabilities effectively in Ukraine and Syria to secure its perceived core interests. With a formidable military as a result of its reforms, the Russian leadership can take greater risks below the level of conflict knowing that NATO and the

---

[9] *Kommersant*, 'Putin: NATO Expansion Dangerous for Russia', 3 December 2019.
[10] President of the Russian Federation, 'The Military Doctrine of the Russian Federation' (in Russian), 5 February 2010, <https://web.archive.org/web/20110504070127/http://www.scrf.gov.ru/documents/33.html>, accessed 28 November 2019.
[11] Keir Giles, *Handbook of Russian Information Warfare*, NATO Defense College Fellowship Manual No. 9 (Rome: NATO Defense College, 2016), <http://www.ndc.nato.int/news/news.php?icode=995>, accessed 18 January 2020.

US may hesitate before taking actions that lead to war with the Russian Federation.

## Hybrid Tactics Backed by Growing Military Capabilities

NATO must adapt to address the new challenges that these tactics present for the Alliance. However, it is critical to underscore that Russia's hybrid tactics can be effective only because they are backed by hard power. In other words, 'hard power underpins hybrid warfare'.[12] Russia uses hybrid tactics when the direct application of military power would be too risky or costly, but its hard power capabilities always loom in the background. This section highlights some of the central concepts that would likely drive the Russian political and military leadership's planning and execution of military operations against NATO.

First, it is important to note that Russia does not think of hybrid tools as being separate from its conventional military capabilities. Instead, the Russian leadership acts within a 'strategic deterrence' framework that encompasses all the instruments of national power spanning from peacetime to wartime, deployed by the Kremlin across a continuous spectrum of competition and conflict between states.[13]

The components of this framework include political (or hybrid) and information warfare (such as the tactics described above), conventional military operations, non-nuclear strategic deterrence, non-strategic nuclear weapons and strategic nuclear weapons. However, unlike the Western concept of deterrence, Russia does not emphasise the nuclear aspect. Instead, the goals of such broad strategic deterrence are to shape the environment during peace and control violence during conflict to convince an adversary that any potential gains from further aggression against Russia are not worth the likely costs.

Second, Russia's concept of strategic deterrence is also structured by a set of phases that extend from normal competition between states to periods of increasing tension and ultimately to open conflict.[14] During each phase, Russian actions will seek to inflict a certain amount of damage designed to

---

[12] Nicole Ng and Eugene Rumer, 'The West Fears Russia's Hybrid Warfare. They're Missing the Bigger Picture', Carnegie Endowment for International Peace, 3 July 2019, <https://carnegieendowment.org/2019/07/03/west-fears-russia-s-hybrid-warfare.-they-re-missing-bigger-picture-pub-79412>, accessed 7 February 2020.

[13] Anya Loukianova Fink, 'The Evolving Russian Concept of Strategic Deterrence: Risks and Responses', *Arms Control Today*, July/August 2017.

[14] Dave Johnson, 'Nuclear Weapons in Russia's Approach to Conflict', Fondation pour la Recherche Stratégique, 28 November 2016, <https://www.frstrategie.org/web/documents/publications/recherches-et-documents/2016/201606.pdf>, accessed 18 January 2020.

advance Moscow's military objectives and, more importantly, create political pressure that allows Russia to end the conflict on Moscow's terms.

Third, these phases or levels of conflict should not be viewed exclusively as sequential, since some, such as information warfare, can persist throughout all phases of the conflict. For example, the Kremlin already employs political warfare to undermine the unity of NATO during peacetime and would certainly continue these efforts during any armed conflict between NATO and Russia with a view to convincing sceptical NATO members of the futility of further support for NATO operations against Russia.

The credibility of each phase is, however, highly dependent on the threat of the damage that the subsequent phase would deliver. Put differently, each phase is meant to communicate to the adversary that, should conflict continue, greater levels of damage will follow. For example, Russia could attack critical infrastructure across NATO and potentially the US with cyber attacks or conventional long-range, precision-guided munitions – part of an evolving concept known as non-nuclear strategic deterrence – to signal the potential political and military cost of continuing the conflict.[15] It is important to realise that during operations that constitute non-nuclear strategic deterrence, the real message coming from the Kremlin would be that if the current level of pain is not enough to bring about some resolution, Russia is prepared to move to the use of non-strategic nuclear weapons and continue along the escalation trajectory.[16]

If Russia and NATO were to move beyond competition short of war into a conventional conflict, the Russian military would seek to capitalise on gains made during the initial period of warfare – a phase Russian strategists see as essential to achieving Russia's political and military goals. This concentration on the opening phases of conflict comes, in part, from the Russian experience during the beginning of the Second World War,

---

[15] Andrei Afanas'evich Kokoshin, 'Strategic Nuclear and Nonnuclear Deterrence: Modern Priorities', *Herald of the Russian Academy of Sciences* (Vol. 84, No. 2, March 2014).

[16] Russian Maritime Studies Institute, 'Maritime Doctrine of the Russian Federation', translated by Anna Davis, 2015, <https://dnnlgwick.blob.core.windows.net/portals/0/NWCDepartments/Russia%20Maritime%20Studies%20Institute/Maritime%20Doctrine%20TransENGrus_FINAL.pdf?sr=b&si=DNNFileManagerPolicy&sig=fqZgUUVRVRrKmSFNMOj%2FNaRNawUoRdhdvpFJj7%2FpAkM%3D>, accessed 18 January 2020; Dave Johnson, 'Russia's Conventional Precision Strike Capabilities, Regional Crises, and Nuclear Thresholds', Livermore Papers on Global Security No. 3, Center for Global Security Research, February 2018, <https://cgsr.llnl.gov/content/assets/docs/Precision-Strike-Capabilities-report-v3-7.pdf>, accessed 18 January 2020.

when the Soviet Union was caught largely off guard by Germany's invasion. It also rests on observations of US operations and an appreciation for modern military capabilities such as long-range, precision-guided munitions, cyber warfare and competition in the information battlespace. Indeed, Russian military leaders calculate that Russia is unlikely to win a prolonged conflict with NATO if the US can deploy forces from the US mainland; as such, Russian strategists likely do not see a conflict with NATO as lasting months, but weeks.[17]

When talking recently about perceived US rapid-strike capabilities coupled with US intentions to create 'colour revolutions', Chief of the Russian General Staff Valery Gerasimov described Russia's approach as one of 'active defence' wherein Russia would take a set of pre-emptive steps to neutralise threats.[18] In adapting to this vision of modern warfare, Russian forces have trained to mobilise quickly and are prepared to employ capabilities rapidly to inflict costs early in a conflict to drive an early political settlement favourable to Russia.

Since at least 2013, this preparation has included extensive, often unannounced, exercises designed to build command-and-control capacity and the ability to deploy forces to any portion of Russia's long border.[19] The goal of such rapid deployment is to achieve dominance quickly in a conflict, including one with NATO, before the conflict takes on a more global scope. These exercises have become increasingly large and complex and, as of 2019, incorporate greater involvement of other militaries, such as the Chinese participation in Exercise *Vostok* 2018.[20]

The advent of long-range precision-guided munitions and advanced electronic warfare within Russia's armed forces, coupled with better use of ISR platforms, also poses a serious challenge to NATO's forces and their ability to maintain appropriate levels of readiness and achieve success during the opening phases of conflict.[21] In a conflict, the Russian military

---

[17] Russian Minister of Defence Sergey Shoigu quoted in Interfax, 'Shoigu Discussed the NATO Implementation of a New Anti-Russian Military Concept', 24 December 2019, <https://www.interfax.ru/world/689196>, accessed 7 February 2020.
[18] Valery Gerasimov, 'The Development of Military Strategy Under Contemporary Conditions. Tasks for Military Science', translated by Harold Orenstein and Timothy Thomas, *Military Review*, November 2019, <https://www.armyupress. army.mil/Journals/Military-Review/Online-Exclusive/2019-OLE/November/ Orenstein-Gerasimov/>, accessed 18 January 2020.
[19] Johan Norberg, 'Training for War: Russia's Military Exercises 2009–2017', FOI-R– 4627–SE, October 2018, <https://www.foi.se/rest-api/report/FOI-R–4627–SE>, accessed 18 January 2020.
[20] *War on the Rocks*, 'Breaking Down Russia's Vostok Exercise', 25 September 2018.
[21] Jeffrey Edmonds and Samuel Bendett, 'Russian Battlefield Awareness and Information Dominance: Improved Capabilities and Future Challenges', Strategy Bridge, 26 February 2019, <https://thestrategybridge.org/the-bridge/2019/2/26/

would challenge the US and NATO's traditional advantage in the use of information on the battlefield. Russian strategists have long recognised the dependence of US and NATO forces on electronically derived information. Russia has therefore sought to address this perceived vulnerability, and electronic warfare is perhaps one of the most successful areas of Russian military modernisation. The Russian military would seek to create what it describes as 'disorganisation' within NATO forces and then to exploit that disorganisation with its own networked forces.[22] Information warfare operations would not only be technical during a time of conflict but would also focus more intently on those political areas where the Russian intelligence services perceive divisions within the Alliance regarding the conflict.

The final point of note is that the strategic deterrence framework is not designed to bring about total victory in the sense commonly conceived by Western military theorists but instead articulates a path to political settlement amenable to Russian interests. The Russian understanding of escalation dominance described above underscores the psychological and political victory Russia would seek in a conflict with NATO.[23] Although the exact components of this victory would depend on the situation, it would arguably include preservation of the Russian regime and an enduring, agreed-upon recognition of Russia's global status as a great power and its regional primacy.

## How NATO Must Respond

As Russian foreign policy under Putin has evolved, Russia has placed greater emphasis on undermining the political cohesion of the Alliance. Russia's increasing use of information warfare and cyber tactics is intended to weaken Western democratic institutions and call into question member states' commitment to collective defence. As underscored in this chapter, however, while the threat of hybrid tactics has grown, these tools are effective only because they are backed by conventional force. NATO must adapt to address the challenges posed by hybrid tactics, but at the same time not lose sight of the conventional threat that Russia poses. This will therefore require a multifaceted response. Given the political and military

russian-battlefield-awareness-and-information-dominance-improved-capabilities-and-future-challenges>, accessed 18 January 2020.
[22] Michael Kofman, 'It's Time to Talk about A2/AD: Rethinking the Russian Military Challenge', *War on the Rocks*, 5 September 2019, <https://warontherocks.com/2019/09/its-time-to-talk-about-a2-ad-rethinking-the-russian-military-challenge/>, accessed 18 January 2020.
[23] Kristin Ven Bruusgaard, 'Russian Strategic Deterrence', *Survival* (Vol. 58, No. 4, 2016).

dynamics described in this chapter, three approaches that NATO must implement are highlighted.

*Deterring Russian Hybrid Tactics*
Russia's greater assertiveness and increasing reliance on hybrid tools such as information warfare and cyber attacks means that sub-Article 5 attacks are likely to be the most frequent challenge that Russia poses to NATO. NATO Allies must therefore invest in building national resilience, which includes hardening critical infrastructure and election systems, increasing financial sector transparency and improving media literacy. Many of these tasks fall to member states, but NATO should work with the EU to set common standards for resilience, including in the cyber realm, and increase NATO–EU coordination in this area.[24] Safeguarding NATO cohesion will also be especially critical in light of Russia's hybrid tactics, which are designed to be ambiguous, to complicate attribution and delay decisions.

*Preventing a Short but Decisive Conflict with Russia*
The asymmetry between Russian and NATO forces in Eastern Europe, along with Russian concepts of operations and the streamlined ability of the Russian leadership to make decisions, means that NATO and the US will have little time to react should a military conflict break out with Russia. Although NATO is not likely to offset the military balance in sheer numbers, increasing readiness, including the readiness of reinforcing conventional forces, would signal both the political will to respond to Russian aggression and the ability to inflict greater costs during conflict, and would therefore undermine the Russian leadership's confidence in carrying out the coercive measures noted earlier. NATO must also focus on streamlining its decision-making, especially in a crisis scenario. This will be critical not only in light of the ambiguity inherent to Russia's hybrid tactics, but also because of Russia's use of deception, or *maskirovka*, to conceal its forces and intentions, and its emphasis on achieving its operational objectives in the earliest days of a campaign.

*Controlling Escalation Dynamics*
The escalation dynamics highlighted above and discussed widely within Russian security circles explicitly link conventional and non-strategic nuclear weapons together in an integrated deterrence and warfighting framework. Therefore, the US and NATO must also begin thinking of the

---

[24] See Douglas Lute and Nicholas Burns, 'NATO at Seventy: An Alliance in Crisis', Harvard Kennedy School, Belfer Center, February 2019.

conventional and nuclear aspects of modern warfare in an integrated fashion. This does not mean that NATO must take the same path as the Russian political and military leadership, but it must avoid stove-piping the discussion of how it would respond to the use of non-strategic weapons on a European battlefield. Actions could include ensuring protocols are in place to access national strategic nuclear capabilities. Given the pace of war expected by Russian strategists, NATO cannot afford to wait until a conflict erupts before undertaking these measures.

## Conclusion

Political observers often mistakenly wonder how a declining power like Russia can continue to pose such a challenge to the US and NATO. The Russian economy is stagnant – it is projected to grow at less than 2% annually until at least 2024; Russia's ageing population is declining, and many of its brightest are leaving to pursue careers elsewhere.[25] According to this logic, the West can simply wait Russia out, making it only a matter of time until the US and Europe can establish a more functional relationship with the Kremlin. Yet as tempting as that logic may be, it is deeply misguided. There is in fact little evidence to suggest that socioeconomic constraints alone will slow Putin's assertive approach or the threat that Russia poses to NATO.

Instead, the Kremlin has shown an ability to push through its own internal challenges, including its economic shortcomings, and play the role of spoiler to what it sees as the West's attempts to keep Russia weak and marginalised. In many ways, Russia has advanced its interests on the cheap: limited military interventions, cyber operations and influence campaigns are relatively inexpensive. In Ukraine and Syria, for example, the Kremlin has employed just enough force to achieve its goals, costing it little economically or in terms of its military capability.

Even in the realm of conventional capability, Russia's internal challenges are unlikely to substantially limit the Russian threat to NATO. For example, factors like a declining population are not projected to hinder the Russian military and its ability. And threats from cyber and nuclear weapons are not significantly affected by demographic decline. Moreover, the broad contours of Russian foreign policy, including the

---

[25] On Russia's economic outlook, see International Monetary Fund, 'Russian Federation: 2019 Article IV Consultation – Press Release; Staff Report', IMF Country Report No. 19/260, August 2019, <https://www.imf.org/en/Publications/CR/Issues/2019/08/01/Russian-Federation-2019-Article-IV-Consultation-Press-Release-Staff-Report-48549>, accessed 7 February 2020. On Russia's 'brain drain', see John Herbst and Sergei Erofeev, *The Putin Exodus: The New Russian Brain Drain* (Washington, DC: Atlantic Council, 2019).

Kremlin's great power ambitions and claim to a sphere of influence in regions along its border, are widely shared across Russian foreign policy and security circles, including among younger professionals, and will persist beyond Putin's time in office.

The challenges that Russia poses to NATO outlined in this chapter, therefore, are likely to persist. Russia's hybrid tactics have received the most attention in recent years, especially since Russia's illegal annexation of Crimea. These tactics seek to erode Alliance cohesion, and the credibility of collective defence, while avoiding the risks and costs associated with direct military confrontation with the US and NATO. Building greater member state resilience to Russian hybrid tactics, therefore, is critical to the continued effectiveness of the Alliance.

But while much attention has been given to Russian hybrid tactics, this chapter has emphasised that they can only be effective because they are backed by conventional forces. The most significant threat that Russia poses to NATO stems from Russia's ability to use hard military power to achieve its political objectives. In other words, 'what Russia does best is conventional war, and if a conflict does not start that way, it is how it always ends'.[26] NATO too, therefore, must continue to hone its conventional capabilities.

Russia is, as the saying goes, playing a relatively weak hand well. It poses a threat to the international order that the US and NATO have stood for since the fall of the Soviet Union and the end of the Cold War. The challenge from Russia is full spectrum, ranging from peacetime political and information warfare to an increasingly capable conventional military backed by the world's largest stockpile of non-strategic and strategic nuclear weapons. Whatever its weaknesses and shortcomings, Russia is a pressing challenge to NATO's survivability and one that will persist into the foreseeable future.

---

[26] Michael Kofman, 'Russian Hybrid Warfare and Other Dark Arts', *War on the Rocks*, 11 March 2016, <https://warontherocks.com/2016/03/russian-hybrid-warfare-and-other-dark-arts/>, accessed 18 January 2020.

# V. NATO'S CHINA CHALLENGE

## JANKA OERTEL

China has for the first time become an important topic in political discussions within NATO. This is very much in line with the overall changing perception of China's global role. Chinese influence is everywhere, and reactions range from hysteria to indifference. The situation calls for a level-headed assessment of China's current priorities and where these clash with interests of the members of the Alliance.

Finding a strategic response to this new geopolitical environment is essential to NATO's continued relevance. While NATO will not operate in Asia any time soon, China's economic and strategic reach is gradually encroaching into NATO territory, and NATO leaders have collectively recognised that they can no longer ignore the implications.[1] Relations with and posture towards an increasingly assertive China will be a key theme for NATO in the coming decades. Especially at a time of transatlantic dissonance and lack of clarity about the future integration of the UK in Europe's security order, devoting the effort necessary to explore emerging challenges may not always be easy, but is certainly essential to ensure an adequate response.

The threats and risks that emanate from China stem from its emergence as a new military superpower, coupled with its strategic ambitions, its relations with Russia and its potential to combine economic power with technological supremacy in various fields, especially in cyberspace. China's military expansion and modernisation are ongoing and have provided ample reason for concern, especially among states in its immediate neighbourhood. While China is currently still a regional military power, its ambition is global, as demonstrated by operations of the People's Liberation Army (PLA) in the Indian Ocean, the

---

[1]  NATO, 'London Declaration', 4 December 2019.

Mediterranean, the Baltic Sea and the Arctic region, which have become the new norm.

## Three Challenges

Since at least the late 1970s, the Chinese leadership has sought to overcome the capability gap between its own armed forces and those of its rivals, acknowledging the need to restructure and rebuild its forces. When Chinese President and Communist Party General Secretary Xi Jinping took over the Central Military Commission (CMC) in 2012, thus becoming commander-in-chief of the PLA, he significantly reinforced modernisation efforts. At the outset of his second five-year term in office in 2017, he called for transforming the PLA by 2035 and building it into a world-class military that can 'fight and win' wars by 2049.[2]

This clear strategic goal is accompanied by an intensifying partnership with Russia, especially in defence technology and military training. Although the Sino-Russian relationship has encountered difficulties in the past, the current trend of increased cooperation is solidifying.[3] Russia remains NATO's first and foremost concern, reinforced by the 2014 invasion of Ukraine, and any collaboration with China that has the potential to strengthen Russia's capabilities or change its force posture has an immediate effect on NATO. Not least, Alliance members on the front lines have begun to worry about Sino-Russian endeavours.

Additionally, China's economic might has increased Beijing's strategic footprint from Tianjin to Lisbon and beyond. Chinese technology companies, especially those in the telecommunications and surveillance fields, are expanding globally, building a digital sphere of influence through non-military means. The heated debate about the use of Chinese vendors to build fifth-generation (5G) mobile telecommunications networks has been the first test of NATO unity when it comes to dealing with China – and it will not be the last.

---

[2] Xi Jinping, 'Secure a Decisive Victory in Building a Moderately Prosperous Society in All Respects and Strive for the Great Success of Socialism with Chinese Characteristics for a New Era', speech delivered at the 19th National Congress of the Communist Party of China, 18 October 2017, <http://www.xinhuanet.com/english/download/Xi_Jinping's_report_at_19th_CPC_National_Congress.pdf>, accessed 7 February 2020.
[3] For example, the new gas pipeline 'Power of Siberia' and ambitious goals for future trade volumes of up to $200 billion by 2024, a figure announced during a visit by Chinese Premier Li Keqiang in Moscow, or the inclusion of Chinese troops in Exercise *Vostok* 2018.

## Military Superpower with Chinese Characteristics
*Guiding Principles and Core Missions*
It is important to emphasise the difference between the PLA and other military forces of similar geopolitical importance or size. The PLA is not intended to serve the Chinese state nor the Chinese people; its core mission is to serve the Chinese Communist Party (CCP). The CCP defines the framework for the development of the armed forces according to its own core interests of solidifying its rule and stabilising its position in power. In line with these interests, the PLA is not only tasked with providing security in the traditional sense, but is also responsible for 'national political security, the people's security and social stability'.[4] In this context, the centre of attention is China's 'territorial integrity', referring primarily to a potential Taiwan independence contingency and the crackdown on 'separatist movements' in Tibet and Xinjiang.[5] Another key focus for the PLA is safeguarding China's growing overseas economic and security interests that extend from the maritime realm to outer space and cyberspace.

*Military Modernisation and Defence Expenditure*
As outlined above, China's military modernisation began decades ago, but has accelerated significantly since 2012. During this time, the PLA has taken important steps towards becoming a leaner, more professional military fit for 21st-century challenges. In his epic three-and-a-half-hour speech at the 19th Party Congress in 2017, President Xi emphasised the importance of these steps and set the parameters for success of this continued effort.[6] In view of the type of war for which the Chinese leadership is preparing, the PLA introduced structural reforms, cutting personnel mainly from the ground forces while adding troops to its air force and navy. Another important development was the establishment of the Strategic Support Force in 2015, responsible for the space, cyber and electronic warfare domains.

Military modernisation is costly, but due to a lack of transparency in Chinese reporting it is difficult to make a definitive assessment of China's defence expenditures. According to the Stockholm International Peace Research Institute (SIPRI), Beijing has significantly increased defence

---

[4] State Council, People's Republic of China (PRC), 'China's National Defense in the New Era', White Paper on Defence, July 2019, <http://english.www.gov.cn/archive/whitepaper/201907/24/content_WS5d3941ddc6d08408f502283d.html>, accessed 7 February 2020.
[5] *Ibid.*
[6] Xi, 'Secure a Decisive Victory in Building a Moderately Prosperous Society in All Respects and Strive for the Great Success of Socialism with Chinese Characteristics for a New Era'.

spending each consecutive year for almost a quarter of a century, with expenditures reaching \$250 billion in 2018 and making China the second-largest spender in the world, surpassed only by the US.[7] These increases reflect the modernisation of military equipment, but as indicated in the 2019 White Paper also underscore the challenges Beijing faces in the current warfighting environment. They are similar to those confronting other advanced militaries and include attracting highly skilled personnel, especially in areas that require technical or IT backgrounds. This is not easy, and requires raising wages and improving work conditions, especially when civilian jobs promise better career opportunities and salaries.[8]

*Techno-Nationalism*

As underscored by Evan Feigenbaum, of the Carnegie Endowment for International Peace, for more than a decade China's current policies have not been new. Instead, they are deeply rooted 'in old strategies, policies, practices, and predilections, as well as deeply held ideologies about the relationship between technology and national power'.[9] China's techno-nationalism describes the relationship as 'intrinsically strategic' and focused on military *and* civilian progress since the 1950s.[10] Investment in research and development is dominated by a focus on capabilities. Nominally private Chinese technology companies have been at the forefront of driving China's innovation ecosystem from 5G to facial recognition and other applications supported by artificial intelligence (AI) and the collection of data. Technologies developed by entrepreneurs from Beijing to Shenzhen – with the help of transfer of know-how from international companies seeking to enter the Chinese market, or through actual indigenous innovation and sometimes through outright theft of intellectual property – are often inherently dual use in nature.[11] This holds especially true in the realms of AI, quantum computing, or drone and

---

[7]   Stockholm International Peace Research Institute (SIPRI), 'World Military Expenditure Grows to \$1.8 Trillion in 2018', 29 April 2019, <https://www.sipri.org/media/press-release/2019/world-military-expenditure-grows-18-trillion-2018>, accessed 7 February 2020.

[8]   Dennis J Blasko, 'Steady as She Goes: China's New Defense White Paper', *War on the Rocks*, 12 August 2019.

[9]   Evan A Feigenbaum, 'The Deep Roots and Long Branches of Chinese Technonationalism', Carnegie Endowment for International Peace, 12 August 2017.

[10]   *Ibid.*

[11]   Elsa Kania, 'In Military-Civil Fusion, China is Learning Lessons from the United States and Starting to Innovate', The Strategy Bridge, 27 August 2019, <https://thestrategybridge.org/the-bridge/2019/8/27/in-military-civil-fusion-china-is-learning-lesssons-from-the-united-states-and-starting-to-innovate>, accessed 7 February 2020.

satellite technology. China has not completed the translation of these technologies into military capabilities, and although the 'Revolution in Military Affairs with Chinese Characteristics', as it is termed in the 2019 White Paper, is well under way, the conclusion in the official document remains that the 'PLA still lags far behind the world's leading militaries' when it comes to modern, information technology-driven warfare.[12] Given China's high ambitions, it is important to pay close attention to Chinese technological developments across the board; in Europe especially, the concerns have too often focused merely on the commercial economic dimension and not on potential or actual military applications.

## Key Developments in Capabilities
### Land Forces
The greatest changes in China's armed forces have occurred in the military command structure and resulted in a relative decline in importance of the PLA Army (PLAA), which had historically been the most influential among the military branches. The former four general departments of the PLAA have been eliminated and functions have been consolidated under the CMC to improve coordination in joint operations. The CMC now holds the overall command, whereas the five theatre commands (East, West, South, North, Central) oversee operations and have invested in joint training and joint exercises. The service headquarters is responsible for force deployment.[13]

The People's Armed Police (PAP), the PLA's 'paramilitary cousin',[14] is now also under the direct control of the CMC.[15] The PAP is responsible for internal security and counterterrorism activities, and is trained for riot control.[16] Such structural changes are partially due to an overall reform process aimed at bringing the PLA in line with Xi's efforts to re-establish Party control over the armed forces and his sweeping anti-corruption efforts. They also represent a response to the new definition of the PLA's mission, placing a much greater emphasis on developing capabilities for force projection beyond China's borders, eliminating bureaucratic

---

[12] State Council, PRC, *China's National Defense in the New Era* (Beijing: Foreign Languages Press, 2019), <http://www.xinhuanet.com/english/2019-07/24/c_138253389.htm>, accessed 7 February 2020.
[13] Bates Gill and Adam Ni, 'China's Sweeping Military Reforms: Implications for Australia', *Security Challenges* (Vol. 15, No. 1, 2019), pp. 33–45.
[14] Joel Wuthnow, 'The Re-Conquerors of Hong Kong? A Primer on China's People's Armed Police', *War on the Rocks*, 23 August 2019.
[15] US–China Economic and Security Review Commission, '2018 Annual Report to Congress', November 2018, p. 215.
[16] It is active in Xinjiang and has been considered to reinforce police forces in Hong Kong during the 2019 protests.

redundancies and turning the PLA into a modern, globally engaged military force. Chinese troops play an active role in UN peacekeeping operations, predominantly on the African continent, and interact directly with military personnel of NATO member states on a daily basis, for example in the context of the UN operation MINUSMA in Mali.[17] These endeavours are also designed to provide the Chinese armed forces with experience in integrated operations and deployments. The impact remains limited so far, but the trajectory is clear. China's military is part of the global security equation and will gradually improve its position far beyond the Indo-Pacific.

## Air and Space Forces

The Chinese air force (PLAAF) has experienced a significant upgrade over the past few years, focusing on offensive as well as defensive capabilities, with a clear aim of building capabilities to operate beyond China's immediate neighbourhood. While the 2019 White Paper states that the size of the active-duty force has remained roughly stable, the upgrade has included investments in modern fighter jets, strategic airlift capabilities and sophisticated missile systems. With the J-20, introduced in 2017, the PLAAF now possesses an indigenously produced fifth-generation stealth fighter jet, which could be adapted for use on the next generation of aircraft carriers currently under construction for the Chinese navy (PLAN).[18] Currently, Chinese air capabilities are mostly of concern within the Indo-Pacific theatre; the projection of carrier capabilities, however, demonstrates China's strategic ambition to operate worldwide.

Chinese officials have stated that by 2020 the PLAAF will be transformed into a strategic force, integrating air and space capabilities.[19] In the space domain, China is putting an emphasis on indigenous capabilities, not only in space exploration, as demonstrated by China's landing of a spacecraft on the far side of the Moon in January 2019, but also in terms of satellite technology. Examples include the BeiDou global navigation system, which was developed for the Chinese military but finds widespread commercial application and is now basically operational

---

[17] Jean-Pierre Cabestan, 'China's Evolving Role as a UN Peacekeeper in Mali', United States Institute of Peace, Special Report 432, September 2018, <https://www.usip.org/sites/default/files/2018-09/sr432-chinas-evolving-role-as-a-un-peacekeeper-in-mali.pdf>, accessed 7 February 2020. Chinese peacekeepers are currently deployed to nine UN missions. For further details, see United Nations Peacekeeping, 'China', <https://peacekeeping.un.org/en/china>, accessed 7 February 2020.
[18] Minnie Chan, 'China's Navy "Set to Pick J-20 Stealth Jets for its Next Generation Carriers"', *South China Morning Post*, 27 August 2019.
[19] Central Military Commission, 'China to Create World-Class Air Force', 12 November 2019, <http://eng.chinamil.com.cn/view/2019-11/12/content_9673613.htm>, accessed 7 February 2020.

worldwide as an alternative to GPS. With 70% of Chinese smartphones already being 'BeiDou ready', replacing GPS for civilian use is a goal that can be achieved by mid-2020,[20] and as Chinese technology companies have a global reach, implications will not be limited to China. The 2019 Annual Report to Congress by the US–China Economic and Security Review Commission assesses that 'China views space as a critical U.S. military and economic vulnerability, and has fielded an array of direct-ascent, cyber, electromagnetic, and co-orbital counterspace weapons capable of targeting nearly every class of U.S. space asset'.[21] This strategic understanding of space provides the Chinese forces with an asymmetric advantage that would cancel out some of the PLA's deficiencies in other military capabilities in a potential conflict scenario with the US and its allies.

*Maritime Forces*
The PLAN has received an enormous amount of attention from the Chinese leadership – and from Western observers. Building a blue water navy is not only key to controlling the waters along China's coastline and to realising China's claims in the South and East China Seas, which has long been at the top of the strategic priorities of the Chinese leadership, but it is also viewed as central to China's prestige and status as a global power. The carrier programmes in particular must be viewed in this context, as they have a particularly strong domestic signalling effect. Additionally, any Taiwan-related scenario is a key element of PLAN training activities.

More relevant from a NATO perspective, however, are the global ambitions of the PLAN, exemplified most directly by the opening of the PLAN's first overseas base in Djibouti on the Horn of Africa in summer 2017. The PLAN already operates in the Indo-Pacific and the waters surrounding Europe with increasing ease and confidence. The most visible example of this was a July 2017 joint exercise with Russian ships in the Baltic Sea. Undoubtedly, China's presence in the Baltic Sea has caused concern in European countries and in this way it has sent a signal to those NATO and European powers that are pursuing freedom of navigation operations (FONOPS) in the South China Sea, which China claims as its exclusive domain.[22]

[20] Werner Pluta, 'China kündigt Fertigstellung von Beidou an', *golem.de*, 28 December 2019, <https://www.golem.de/news/satellitennavigationssystem-china-kuendigt-fertigstellung-von-beidou-an-1912-145761.html>, accessed 7 February 2020.
[21] US–China Economic and Security Review Commission, '2019 Annual Report to Congress', November 2019, p. 360.
[22] David Martin, 'Chinese Warships en Route to Baltic Sea', *Deutsche Welle*, 18 July 2017, <https://www.dw.com/en/chinese-warships-en-route-to-baltic-sea/a-39735964>, accessed 7 February 2020.

*Strategic Support Force*
The most recent result of the restructuring process was the creation of the
PLA Strategic Support Force (PLASSF) in 2015. The PLASSF is now
responsible for China's space, cyber, electronic and psychological warfare
capabilities. It provides the PLA with command, control, communications,
computers, intelligence, surveillance and reconnaissance (C4ISR)
support.[23] It collects and delivers information, including through 'space-
based surveillance, satellite relay and communications, and telemetry,
tracking, and navigation'.[24] These capabilities are used by all military
branches, with applications ranging from long-range missiles to traditional
battlespace operations on the ground or on the high seas.[25] The PLASSF's
cyber responsibilities include cyber attack and cyber espionage in the
military realm and are designed to exploit an opponent's vulnerabilities in
the information domain.

China's cyber capabilities, broadly defined, probably present the most
imminent threat to NATO security, and NATO must build a thorough
understanding of the PLA's capabilities in this realm.

## Implications for NATO
China's vastly enhanced military capabilities have direct implications for
NATO. Combined with China's economic prowess, they change the
geostrategic environment for the Alliance – both indirectly, via the
strengthening of the Beijing–Moscow axis, and directly, as the 5G debate
demonstrates. Discussions at the NATO Leaders' Meeting in London in
December 2019, and the preceding review process, can be seen as early
indicators of what will likely become a much broader debate about
NATO's relations with China in the years to come.

*China–Russia Relations*
China used to be fairly isolated in terms of security cooperation, its only
formal ally being North Korea, and its armed forces have little to no actual
combat experience. In recent years, however, Beijing and Moscow have
invested in strengthening their partnership – politically, economically and

---

[23] Janka Oertel, Andrew Small and Amy Studdart, 'The Liberal Order in the
Indo-Pacific', German Marshall Fund of the United States, Asia Programme Report,
13 April 2018, p. 22.
[24] US–China Economic and Security Review Commission, '2019 Annual Report to
Congress', p. 292.
[25] John Costello and Joe McReynolds, 'China's Strategic Support Force: A Force for a
New Era', Institute for National Strategic Studies, China Strategic Perspectives (No. 13,
October 2018), p. 18.

especially in the realm of security and defence. Russia's 'pivot to Asia' was reinforced in the aftermath of the annexation of Crimea in 2014 and the subsequent deterioration of Moscow's relations with the West. Both sides have made strong public statements about the 'friendship' between the countries and the close personal ties between Russian President Vladimir Putin and President Xi.[26] Their diplomatic and political support for each other plays out especially within the framework of the UN Security Council and the broader UN system.[27] The economic dimension of the relationship does not match the positive rhetoric, however. The discrepancies in economic prowess are obvious and have led to a highly asymmetric relationship in this area.[28]

Most important from a NATO perspective is China–Russia cooperation in the defence and security realm. Since 1989, Russian arms sales have formed the backbone of China's military modernisation 'by coincidence, rather than design',[29] as Russia needed a market for its arms industry after the collapse of the Soviet Union and China was cut off from Western sources by the arms embargo imposed in response to the Tiananmen Square massacre carried out by PLA forces. The level of trust initially remained comparatively low due to decades of conflict and unresolved border questions, and Russia primarily provided China with outdated or at least older technologies.[30] This has changed: in 2015 Russia agreed to sell advanced systems to China, including two dozen Su-35 and several S-400 surface-to-air missile systems. While the Chinese leadership underlines the importance of close ties with Moscow, which according to the 2019 White Paper play 'a significant role in maintaining global strategic stability',[31] China is steadily building its indigenous capacities and is now surpassing Russia in some key technologies. Thus, Beijing has become more interested in acquiring advanced components and human resources from Russia than in importing entire weapon systems. As noted by Samuel Bendett and Elsa Kania, 'Russia's skilled engineers and mathematicians are

[26] *Reuters,* 'China's Xi Awards "Best Friend" Putin Friendship Medal, Promises Support', 8 June 2018.
[27] An overview of the veto record can be accessed at <https://research.un.org/en/docs/sc/quick>, accessed 27 February 2020.
[28] According to the World Bank, Russia's GDP reached $1.658 trillion in 2018, roughly equivalent to that of Italy, while China's GDP reached $13.608 trillion.
[29] Siemon T Wezeman, 'China, Russia and the Shifting Landscape of Arms Sales', SIPRI, 5 July 2017, <https://www.sipri.org/commentary/topical-backgrounder/2017/china-russia-and-shifting-landscape-arms-sales>, accessed 7 February 2020.
[30] Ethan Meick, 'China-Russia Military-to-Military Relations: Moving Toward a Higher Level of Cooperation', US–China Economic and Security Review Commission Staff Report, 20 March 2017, p. 12.
[31] State Council, PRC, 'China's National Defense in the New Era'.

a valuable resource for tech and defense industry giants that are hungry for talent and faced with increasingly unfavorable conditions in the United States and Europe'.[32] On 23 December 2019, Putin signed a decree declaring 2020–21 the 'Year of Scientific, Technical and Innovation Cooperation' with China.[33] Chinese technology companies already have a strong foothold in the Russian market, telecommunications giant Huawei being a special case in point.

Despite a degree of unease that persists in Moscow with regard to the balance of the relationship,[34] cooperating with China in research and development brings benefits and necessary financing to the Russian technology sector.[35] It is often argued that the Russia–China relationship is nothing but a marriage of convenience, and while this is largely true, it does not mean that the relationship cannot and will not last. The way in which bilateral relations have developed over the past few years warrants a degree of caution, especially in the defence realm: military cooperation has significantly increased, while joint training and exercises have enabled the Russian and Chinese militaries to become 'more familiar with each other'.[36] While the two nations have not formed a classic alliance, the potential of the relationship is enormous and should not be underestimated. Europe and the US can currently do little to change the trajectory of the relationship, but NATO members and partners need to monitor this development closely and identify its potential impact on Allied security.

*The 5G Battle*
While China–Russia relations will be on the long-term 'watch list' for NATO strategists, and it is far from certain how they will evolve, the growing strategic competition between the US and China has already become a central topic of discussion in NATO. The first, and most obvious, example of this has been the battle over the 5G infrastructure.

---

[32] Samuel Bendett and Elsa B Kania, 'China, Russia Deepen Technological Ties', *Defense One*, 4 October 2019.
[33] *Tass*, 'Russia, China Discussing Key Projects for Year of Scientific Cooperation', 25 December 2019.
[34] Hiroyuki Akita, 'China and Russia Build Anti-US 'Axis', but Moscow has Concerns', *Nikkei Asian Review*, 11 July 2018.
[35] Council on Foreign Relations, 'China and Russia: Collaborators or Competitors?', 1 November 2018, <https://www.cfr.org/blog/china-and-russia-collaborators-or-competitors>, accessed 7 February 2020.
[36] Dmitri Trenin, 'How Cozy is Russia and China's Military Relationship?', Carnegie Moscow Center, 19 November 2019; Alexander Gabuev, 'Why Russia and China Are Strengthening Security Ties', Carnegie Moscow Center, 24 September 2018.

The fifth generation of mobile communication networks will produce nothing less than a digital revolution. It will allow for low-latency, high-speed connections that enable civilian applications from autonomous driving to remote surgery and will also have a significant effect on military communications, reconnaissance capabilities and automated warfare. Many of the applications that 5G can enable are still being developed. The telecommunications infrastructure, which will be rolled out over the next few years, will form the backbone on which these new applications will be built and is thus of critical importance.

Through the interplay of new hardware and advanced software, the vendor of the equipment will play a much greater role in maintenance of the new systems. Manufacturers will be responsible for critical security updates and will necessarily continue to have access to the network. The leading companies currently supplying comprehensive 5G solutions are European and Chinese: Nokia, Ericsson, Huawei and ZTE (South Korea's Samsung also being an important player). The two Chinese companies have been largely excluded from the US market due to security concerns ranging from espionage to potential disruptions of service. In Europe, both companies, especially Huawei, play a leading role in the existing 3G/4G infrastructure and were also expected to provide 5G services on a massive scale. This raised alarms in Washington over the potential economic, technological and strategic influence that Beijing would gain by extending a digital sphere of influence into the heart of NATO territory.

US Vice President Mike Pence prominently raised the issue at the 2019 Munich Security Conference, pushing NATO to place 5G on its agenda. Pence underlined US expectations vis-à-vis its partners: 'The United States has also been very clear with our security partners on the threat posed by Huawei and other Chinese telecom companies ... America is calling on all our security partners to be vigilant and to reject any enterprise that would compromise the integrity of our communications technology or our national security systems'.[37] On a visit to Budapest in 2019, Secretary of State Mike Pompeo reiterated that the choices made with regard to 5G networks would directly affect US military cooperation with the Alliance and could have an effect on the future of interoperability within NATO.[38]

---

[37] Mike Pence, 'Remarks by Vice President Pence at the 2019 Munich Security Conference', speech given in Munich, February 2019, <https://www.whitehouse.gov/briefings-statements/remarks-vice-president-pence-2019-munich-security-conference-munich-germany/>, accessed 19 January 2020.

[38] Lesley Wroughton and Gergely Szakacs, 'Pompeo Warns Allies Huawei Presence Complicates Partnership with US', *Reuters*, 11 February 2019.

The forcefulness with which Washington pursued its campaign among its European allies is unprecedented in recent years: over the course of 2019, countless official delegations visited European capitals, exchanged notes with the EU and tried to shape public discourse, with mixed success.

Among Allies on NATO's eastern flank, the security and interoperability argument – or the fear that the US might renege on its Article 5 commitments – proved reasonably effective. Estonia, Poland and Romania committed in one way or another to exclude Chinese vendors from building their 5G infrastructure. Norway's Nortel and Denmark's TDC – the largest mobile operators in the countries – followed suit. In Germany, the Netherlands and Italy fierce domestic discussions are taking place – in Germany with serious anti-US undertones.[39] The emotional debate over the issue underlines existing rifts in the transatlantic relationship, which are reinforced by changes in the geopolitical realities of the 21st century that are manifested by the growing importance of the economic relationship with China for most Allies.

The latest leaders' meeting in London serves as an indication that 5G represents just the beginning of a new conversation about China within NATO. Discussions underscored the need to address, as the Declaration stated, the 'breadth and scale of new technologies to maintain our technological edge, while preserving our values and norms. … NATO and Allies, within their respective authority, are committed to ensuring the security of our communications, including 5G, recognising the need to rely on secure and resilient systems'.[40] 5G is the first test case for NATO unity when it comes to resisting China's economic influence.

*NATO's China Review*
Prior to the London meeting, NATO quietly undertook a review of its relations with China.[41] The process was initiated by Washington and can

---

[39] Janka Oertel, 'Germany Chooses China Over the West', *Foreign Policy*, 21 October 2019; Janka Oertel, 'Europe and China after Brexit: The 5G Question', European Council on Foreign Relations, 19 December 2019, <www.ecfr.eu/article/commentary_europe_and_china_after_brexit_the_5g_question>, accessed 7 February 2020.
[40] NATO, 'London Declaration Issued by the Heads of State and Government Participating in the Meeting of the North Atlantic Council in London, 3–4 December 2019', <https://www.nato.int/cps/en/natohq/official_texts_171584.htm>, accessed 7 February 2020.
[41] Fabrice Pothier, 'How Should NATO Respond to China's Growing Power?', International Institute for Strategic Studies, 12 September 2019.

be seen as directly connected to changes in US policy reflecting the increased competition presented by China. European Allies agreed to debate the strategic challenges posed by China's new global role only after significant pressure by the US; France in particular hesitated to debate China within the NATO context.[42] NATO's comprehensive analysis covered the expanding China–Russia relationship as well as Chinese investments in strategic infrastructure in Europe, especially in ports, which could be relevant to NATO deployment in case of conflict.

The results of this process remain defensive in nature but represent a first step towards recognition within NATO of China's future role from cyberspace to the Arctic.

## Conclusion

The US has recognised the challenge emanating from China and shifted its priorities accordingly, a process that will naturally require European NATO members to contribute more to European security as US focus shifts further east. For Europe, China remains for the most part still an abstract military challenge, but the changing understanding of security must find its way into defence planning quickly to avoid a rude awakening. Technology is the battlespace for future warfare, and NATO must take China's holistic approach to national security very seriously. Unlike in previous centuries, when security concerns focused on traditional military equipment from ships to aircraft, the means to compete will be defined to a far greater extent in the cyber and economic domains. Export controls will acquire new significance. The boundaries between technology for civilian and military use have already become blurred and dual-use regulation may not always be the most feasible and reasonable way to manage this challenge. NATO members should revisit all available instruments and make them fit for purpose. The difficulty will lie in preserving economic relationships with China for mutual benefit while maintaining and developing the capabilities necessary for national security.

NATO's role in the new geopolitical environment of the 21st century will naturally undergo significant changes. The Alliance can serve as the venue for in-depth exchange and debate about how this world can be shaped. An important lesson of 2019 is that the US will not be able to pursue this path alone. At a time when economic power is of particularly high importance, Europe's contribution to North Atlantic security is growing and strong transatlantic relations will

---

[42] Robbie Gramer, 'Trump Wants NATO's Eyes on China', *Foreign Policy*, 20 March 2019; author's conversations with senior policymakers.

be key. China is an authoritarian power challenging the values that are core to NATO's existence: freedom, human rights and democracy. By acknowledging the new realities and taking China's ambitions seriously, European powers within NATO can contribute to building a credible defence architecture for the future – especially in cyberspace. NATO has always been designed to defend the Allies against military threats as well as systemic rivals. While NATO is likely not the right institution to defend 'democracy' as a concept, it is inherently designed to defend democracies.

# VI. NATO AND ITS SOUTHERN FLANK

## ZIYA MERAL

Adversaries rarely target attacks on the opponent's strongholds or undertake operations where expected. Instead, they seek out weak points where defence and security are often overlooked, unprepared or insufficiently considered in planning and preparations. This pattern is evident in the way terror groups choose their targets and the way peer adversaries attempt to increase and exploit each other's weaknesses to maximise their own interests and achievements.

NATO would do well to consider this. The Alliance has certainly demonstrated tremendous adaptability to changing threats since Russia's 2014 invasion of Crimea, from increasing its focus on countering adversaries' misinformation campaigns and their anti-access and area-denial operations to further extending its own capabilities for interoperability and rapid deployment. These advances were promoted by a deep threat perception shared among the countries in NATO's northern and eastern regions, which have clear awareness of how the observed patterns of Russian activities present considerable direct and indirect risks of destabilising the region. Yet NATO has continued to pay relatively less attention to its southern borders – its soft underbelly – even while recent developments across the Balkans and the Aegean and Mediterranean shores raise serious questions about NATO priorities and strategic thinking.

This chapter aims to summarise key trends and developments that affect countries on NATO's southern borders, as well as vulnerabilities that could undermine its unity and stability. It starts by briefly examining external threats facing the Alliance and the concerns of members located in the south, before turning to internal dynamics that are straining the Alliance and providing adversaries with ample opportunities to weaken collective defence. The chapter concludes by identifying the implications for NATO and calling for a deeper and more meaningful engagement with the south beyond strategic-level acknowledgements of its importance.

## All Is Not Well in the Troubled South

For the past decade, two issues have dominated discussion of the concerns of southern members of the Alliance and the external challenges they face: terrorism and irregular migration. Both elicit strong public feelings and reactions and have played a larger than warranted role in shaping the political direction of many governments across the Alliance. Regardless of whether these threats actually pose an existential risk to, or an unmanageable burden on, NATO members, both are undoubtedly complex phenomena that will continue to present serious challenges. Combating the underlying conditions that drive terrorism and irregular migration in the region requires substantial investment and involvement by local, regional and global actors and often far exceeds NATO's mandate and capabilities. Nevertheless, they do touch on NATO's mandate to support the defence and security of its members, and both require looking beyond short-term fixes. In many ways, NATO is already implementing such responses.

At the operational level, NATO has supported the Global Coalition against the Islamic State (ISIS) since October 2016 by providing AWACS (Airborne Warning and Control System) intelligence flights,[1] and has undertaken training programmes to strengthen Iraqi forces since October 2018.[2] In 2016, NATO also expanded the remit of Operation *Active Endeavour* – a maritime counterterrorism initiative in the Mediterranean Sea launched following the September 2001 attacks on the US – into a much wider 'non-Article 5' maritime security framework called Operation *Sea Guardian*.[3] Beyond counterterrorism, the operation's mandate includes providing safe passage and information to civilian vessels, and building maritime capacity across the region.

At the political and strategic levels, NATO has a tradition of engaging with countries in the south. The Mediterranean Dialogue (MD) established in 1994 fostered political dialogue and practical cooperation with seven countries in the region: Algeria, Egypt, Israel, Jordan, Mauritania, Morocco and Tunisia.[4] The Istanbul Cooperation Initiative (ICI) was established in

---

[1]  NATO, 'NATO AWACS Surveillance Aircraft Support to the Counter ISIS Coalition', Factsheet, December 2018, <https://www.nato.int/nato_static_fl2014/assets/pdf/pdf_2018_12/20181210_1812-factsheet-awacs-isil-en.pdf>, accessed 19 January 2020.

[2]  NATO, 'NATO Mission Iraq', <https://www.nato.int/cps/en/natohq/topics_166936.htm>, accessed 19 January 2020.

[3]  NATO, 'Operation Active Endeavour (Archived)', <https://mc.nato.int/missions/operation-active-endeavour>, accessed 19 January 2020; NATO, 'Operation Sea Guardian', <https://mc.nato.int/missions/operation-sea-guardian>, accessed 19 January 2020.

[4]  NATO, 'Mediterranean Dialogue', <https://www.nato.int/cps/en/natohq/topics_52927.htm>, accessed 19 January 2020.

2004 to extend NATO engagement into the Gulf region, with Bahrain, Qatar, Kuwait and the UAE joining the initiative.[5] Members of the ICI and MD send officers to courses at the NATO Defense College in Rome; members of the ICI also contributed to NATO operations in Afghanistan and Libya in 2011. NATO has also cooperated with the African Union (AU) since 2002, providing operational support to AU missions in Sudan and Somalia. In November 2019, the two organisations signed a new agreement calling for closer collaboration,[6] a recommendation made at the 2016 Warsaw Summit.[7]

NATO has also taken organisational steps to engage with complex social, political, defence and security issues in the south. The creation in 2017 of the NATO Strategic Direction – South (NSD – S) Hub similarly reflects NATO's recognition at the Warsaw Summit of the need to deepen mutual understanding and strategic partnerships in the region.[8] The hub is intended to provide a forum for engagement with civil society and experts from the Middle East/North Africa, the Sahel and sub-Saharan Africa.

There are clear benefits to increasing understanding of these regions among NATO Allies, deepening conversations with partners and collaborating with local and international non-governmental and government organisations in delivering development aid and conflict prevention and countering violent extremism projects. Yet the legacy of such initiatives has been varied and, in some cases, there has clearly been a lack of momentum and adequate attention. For example, it remains unclear whether the NSD – S is sufficiently resourced given its substantial portfolio and whether its importance is recognised widely across the NATO leadership and structures. Similarly, engagements with the MD and ICI countries have been complicated by serious questions over their

---

[5] NATO, 'Istanbul Cooperation Initiative (ICI)', <https://www.nato.int/cps/en/natohq/topics_52956.htm>, accessed 19 January 2020.

[6] NATO, 'NATO-African Union Plan Closer Collaboration', 4 November 2019, <https://www.nato.int/cps/en/natohq/news_170512.htm>, accessed 19 January 2020.

[7] The Warsaw Summit communiqué states: 'NATO's cooperation with the African Union (AU) encompasses operational, logistic and capacity building support, as well as support for the operationalisation of the African Standby Force, including through exercises, and tailor-made training, in accordance with the AU's requests to NATO. We look forward to further strengthening and expanding our political and practical partnership with the AU, so we are better able to respond together to common threats and challenges'. NATO, 'Warsaw Summit Communiqué Issued by the Heads of State and Government Participating in the Meeting of the North Atlantic Council in Warsaw, 8–9 July 2016', <https://www.nato.int/cps/en/natohq/official_texts_133169.htm>, accessed 19 January 2020.

[8] NATO, 'NATO Strategic Direction South Hub Inaugurated', 5 September 2017, <https://www.nato.int/cps/en/natohq/news_146835.htm>, accessed 19 January 2020.

pursuit of, or failure to pursue, democracy, human rights and good governance norms – although the partnership with ICI members has at least been more focused and dynamic. It is difficult to assess what positive impact NATO has had through its limited high-level interactions with these countries or even whether NATO has presented a clear, unified message about what it expects to achieve from such engagements.

It might appear, then, that such attempts to widen NATO engagement are adding undue pressure on the Alliance and stretching its mandate. However, Russian activities to NATO's south suggest a gradual exploitation of its soft strategic underbelly. These activities span a broad geographic area, from the Black Sea to the Aegean and Balkans, to the Levant and Libya. With its operations in Syria, Russia has not only positioned itself as a power broker that cannot be ignored; but it has also used the theatre as a training ground for thousands of military and security personnel and contractors to gain combat experience and experiment with and showcase new Russian capabilities. No European country, or NATO as a whole, can currently match the battle experience that Russian troops have gained in Syria. Russia's lease of the Syrian port of Tartus since 2017 and its subsequent decision to invest some $500 million in its development highlight Russian ambitions to establish an advanced naval presence in the Mediterranean. NATO must take this into account in its response to Russia's pursuit of greater dominance in the Black Sea.[9] However, Russian reach and activities are not limited to hard power and its military posture: it also seeks to expand Russian soft-power influence and destabilise national governments by deepening social and political fault lines – as has been seen in the Western Balkans, for example.[10]

Libya offers a good example of where NATO's mandate overlaps significantly with both the concerns of its southern members regarding migration, trafficking and terrorism and the concerns of its northern and eastern members regarding Russian ambitions and activities. In 2019, Russia deployed contractors and special forces to aid the campaign by Khalifa Haftar to take control of Tripoli from the UN-backed government,[11] which at the time of writing in early 2020 remained vulnerable – although Turkey also began deploying military personnel to

---

[9]  Henry Foy, 'Russia to Invest $500m in Syrian Port of Tartus', *Financial Times*, 17 December 2019.

[10]  For a good background to Russian activities in the Western Balkans, see Dimitar Bechev, *Rival Power: Russia in Southeast Europe* (New Haven, CT: Yale University Press, 2017).

[11]  Busra Nur Bilgic Cakmak, 'Russia Sends Fighters to Up Haftar's Forces in Libya', *Anadolu Agency*, 7 January 2020, <https://www.aa.com.tr/en/africa/russia-sends-fighters-to-up-haftars-forces-in-libya/1694935>, accessed 19 January 2020.

Tripoli in January 2020 to help in its defence.[12] Russia's goals in Libya clearly follow the patterns of its aims in Syria. Control of Libya would give Russia new ports and economic opportunities; it would also enhance its position as a power broker in a critical geographical hub where so many NATO member states and regional countries have complex interests. It must be asked where the current situation leaves NATO. While Italy was the obvious Alliance candidate to play a leading role in stabilising Libya, its ability to do so has been undermined by its own political weaknesses.[13]

## State of the Alliance and Disagreements Within NATO

Clearly, the current operating environment poses challenging questions for NATO. Equally important, however, is the deepening and worrying pattern of strategic divergence and bilateral tensions among its member states, which could easily weaken the Alliance's resilience and provide substantial opportunities for Russian exploitation.

### Turkish Foreign Policy

First among these is the direction of Turkish foreign policy. Although the obvious value and importance of the Alliance means that leaving NATO is not considered an option in Ankara, Turkish leaders increasingly sense that Turkey cannot rely on NATO's support when differences occur, while some member states are seen as actively undermining Turkey's security and stability. This point becomes clear for anyone who engages with Turkish officials. Policymakers in Ankara still complain about the responses of NATO leaders and officials to the attempted coup and the downing of the Russian jet in 2015, the arming of Kurdish militants at war with Turkey and the ending of Patriot missile deployments from Turkey by some NATO allies. Yet Ankara's handling of these issues and its, at times, justifiable resentment, has been far from productive. Buying Russian missile systems has not filled the capability gap in air-defence systems, as they are limited in performance and not connected to larger radar infrastructure; instead, it has made Turkey more vulnerable to Russian pressure and caused it to lose its place in NATO's F-35 project, risking the imposition of US sanctions and loss of future export licences granted by NATO countries in the process.

All this demonstrates that Turkey's relationship with Russia is based on a toxic paradox. On the one hand, it is necessary for Turkey to engage with

---

[12] *BBC News*, 'Libya Conflict: Turkey Sends Troops to Shore Up UN-Backed Government', 6 January 2020.

[13] See Crispian Balmer, "Italian Foreign Policy Flounders Amidst Libyan Blunders', *Reuters,* 9 January 2020.

Russia on Syria, the economy, trade and energy issues, and this overlaps with Turkey's increasing distrust of NATO and the US and the ideological appeal of religious nationalism and strategic autonomy. On the other hand, Ankara knows all too well that Moscow is a strategic competitor rather than a reliable ally, and that the risk of falling out with Russia over their respective foreign policy priorities is real – a fact which underscores the fundamental importance of NATO for Turkey. But this alone provides a superb opportunity for Russia to weaken Turkey's relationship with NATO, which in turn complicates collective deterrence and cohesion along its southern flank, where Turkey plays a crucial role across a wide portfolio from the Black Sea to the Balkans, the Aegean, Mediterranean, Syria and Iraq. Russia does not want Turkey to leave NATO, but to remain in the Alliance and perpetuate strained relations that Moscow can manipulate.

*US–Turkey Relations*

The second, and related, issue is the deepening rift between the US and Turkey. Washington's anger towards Turkey, most specifically towards President Recep Tayyip Erdogan, goes beyond today's deeply polarised American politics and can be seen throughout US political groups, government bodies and think tanks.[14] In addition to disputes arising from Turkey's purchase of Russian missiles, US and Turkish policies regarding northeast Syria remain irreconcilable.

In 2017, President Barack Obama's administration decided to fight ISIS by arming the Syrian Kurdish People's Protection Units (YPG), which are linked to the Kurdistan Workers' Party (PKK), a Turkish- and US-designated terrorist group. The administration did so without making an overall commitment to the Syrian operation and without pushing for a peace settlement between Turkey and the PKK. Thereafter, it was only a matter of time before Turkey launched military operations to stop the YPG from creating a territorial entity within Syria, along the Turkish border. The failure of efforts to prevent this has both intensified the suffering of civilians in northeast Syria and stimulated great anger in Turkey and the US towards each other.

Turkey still lacks a clear end goal beyond denying PKK-related groups territory in Syria. It has also failed to establish a new vision for addressing Kurdish grievances. In this way, its incursion into Syria in late 2019 paradoxically weakens Turkey's long-term security: it provides a short-term military fix for a long-term strategic challenge. Yet its national

---

[14] For an up-to-date background on US–Turkey relations, see Philip Gordon and Amanda Sloat, 'The Dangerous Unravelling of the US-Turkish Alliance', *Foreign Affairs*, 10 January 2020.

security concerns are real, and the historic rift between the US and Turkey will not be patched up soon. Perhaps ironically, the personal relationship between Trump and Erdogan seems to be the only remaining factor preventing a complete collapse of bilateral relations.

*Cyprus*
The third issue concerns Cyprus, which is marked by a frozen partition and repeated diplomatic initiatives that have been largely futile since the southern part of the island joined the EU in 2004, despite the absence of a solution to the territorial dispute with Turkey. This situation is no longer sustainable. The discovery of energy resources has raised the stakes for the islanders and their guarantors. The dispute is further escalated by the alliance formed between Israel, Egypt and Greece over Cyprus,[15] all of which have their own grievances against Turkey. For Turkey, too, Cyprus is emerging as an important strategic factor in its military presence in the Mediterranean, with talks of establishing a Turkish naval base on the island.[16]

The situation in Cyprus is also once again fuelling the historic tensions between Greece and Turkey. The recent Turkish deal with the UN-backed government in Tripoli, under which Turkey believes it can extend its reach in disputed waters and dispatch vessels to search for energy and intimidate rivals, is causing widespread alarm in Greece.[17] NATO has played a key part in containing the fallout from such tensions between Greece and Turkey. An article by experts in the CSIA European Security Working Group called 'Instability and Change on NATO's Southern Flank' included the following worrying observation in this regard:

> one need only take a cursory glance at the southern flank today to see how radically the situation has changed. On the bilateral level, US relations with both Greece and Turkey have seriously deteriorated. On the alliance level, Greece has withdrawn from the military structures of NATO, while Turkey is threatening to reduce her commitment and could at some point even drop out entirely. Meanwhile, the Cyprus issue continues to fester, poisoning relations between Greece and Turkey and exacerbating tensions over other

---

[15]    On energy projects bringing them together, see Hagar Hosny, 'Egypt Unruffled by EastMed Pipeline Project', *Al Monitor*, 20 January 2020, <https://www.al-monitor.com/pulse/originals/2020/01/egypt-israel-greece-cyprus-east-med-pipeline-gas-deals-worry.html>, accessed 7 February 2020.

[16]    *Daily Sabah*, 'Turkey Plans to Establish Naval Base in Cyprus', 25 December 2019, <https://www.dailysabah.com/politics/2019/12/25/turkey-plans-to-establish-naval-base-in-cyprus>, accessed 7 February 2020.

[17]    See *TRT World*, 'Why is Turkey Taking up its Libya Deal With the UN?', 2 January 2020, <https://www.trtworld.com/turkey/why-is-turkey-taking-up-its-libya-deal-with-the-un-32667>, accessed 7 February 2020.

issues in the Aegean. Lastly, domestic trends in both countries raise troubling questions about the long-term viability of their democratic institutions.[18]

This description is familiar today; however, the article was written in 1978. NATO has been a core factor in containing fallout between the two nations. However, given Turkey–US tensions and the other developments listed above, the risk of an escalation over Cyprus that leads to a deeper crisis between Turkey and Greece is very real for NATO – especially in view of Russian activities to hasten their manifestation.

*The Wider Context*

These developments – in Turkish foreign policy, bilateral relations between the US and Turkey and tensions over Cyprus – do not occur in a vacuum. Trump's administration continues its confusing relationship with NATO and with Europe as a whole; it is similarly difficult to discern a coherent and long-term US policy towards NATO's southern flank. Meanwhile, the perception of China as an adversary pervades defence and foreign policy thinking across party lines in Washington. In the age of 'great power competition' and strain on those frameworks and institutions that have previously maintained peace, medium-sized regional powers are going on the offensive. They believe they must assert themselves and take risks in the current geopolitical environment.

Turning to domestic considerations, countries across Europe and North America are experiencing a resurgence of far-right extremism and a return to notions of 'White Christian Civilisation vs the Other', which has fuelled disturbing political developments.[19] These movements have tended to find their voice in 'strong man' figures across the world who promise greater national power and a 'pure' society at the expense of personal rights, freedoms and checks and balances. All these trends fundamentally undermine multilateralism and the values that underpin the international rules-based order in general and NATO's mission specifically.

This explains why the Kremlin is promoting its credentials as the 'defender' of Christian civilisation and of minorities in the Middle East and the Balkans,[20] and why Moscow can easily build ties with far-right groups

---

[18] CSIA European Security Working Group, 'Instability and Change on NATO's Southern Flank', *International Security* (Vol. 3, No. 3, Winter 1978–79), pp. 150–77.

[19] See Andrea Mammone, 'Europe's Far Right Seems Determines to Hijack Christianity in its Bid for Power', *The Independent*, 13 January 2019.

[20] See Lesia Shymko, 'The Weaponization of Religion: How the Kremlin is Using Christian Fundamentalism to Advance Moscow's Agenda', *day.kyiv.ua*, 5 September 2019, <https://day.kyiv.ua/en/article/day-after-day/weaponization-religion-how-kremlin-using-christian-fundamentalism-advance>, accessed 19 January 2020.

in the West,[21] garner sympathy for its brutal military campaign in Syria and play off NATO member states against each other. At the moment, Russia has variable working relations with both Greece and Turkey, a direct and indirect presence in Cyprus, maintains good relations with Israel and Egypt and supports Libya's 'dictator-in-waiting', Khalifa Haftar. NATO must deepen its proactive approach in the Mediterranean, or Russia will extend its reach from Tartus to Tripoli, thus gaining sea routes from the Black Sea – where it has increasing dominance – to the Mediterranean and expanding its role as a 'peace broker'.

## Implications for NATO

Fortunately, as noted earlier, NATO has taken fresh and promising steps to increase its presence in the Black Sea, acknowledged the necessity of engaging more robustly in the issues relating to its southern flank, adapted significantly to meet the challenges presented by new Russian capabilities and tactics and strengthened its defence and political posture overall. Moreover, NATO's Secretary General has proven himself a superb statesman capable of promoting cohesion among Allies.[22] NATO's Military Committee is also turning its attention to NATO's southern flank – specifically, to ongoing work strands and opportunities for enhanced cooperation with partners with common interests in the region, such as the AU, the EU and the UN.[23] NATO has also moved quickly to welcome North Macedonia as a new member – after a 20-year wait – following the resolution of the dispute with Greece over the country's name. As a result, North Macedonia will soon become the Alliance's 30th member.

NATO has further demonstrated wisdom in its response to the current strategic chaos in US foreign policy; in its handling of Turkish attempts to assert strategic independence, as well as ambitions of France; in containing tensions between Greece and Turkey; in encouraging higher investment in defence across its members; and in finding ways to balance the complex web of relations it shares with the EU. Each of these achievements demonstrate that the 70-year-old organisation is neither 'brain dead', as described by French President Emmanuel Macron in the run-up to the

---

[21] See Anton Shekhovtsov, *Russia and the Western Far Right* (London: Routledge, 2017).

[22] In fact, Jens Stoltenberg received the 'Diplomat of the Year' award from *Foreign Policy Magazine* in 2019. See NATO, 'NATO Secretary General Accepts Foreign Policy's "Diplomat of the Year" Award', 12 November 2019.

[23] NATO, '182nd Military Committee in Chiefs of Defence Session – NATO Headquarters, Brussels, Belgium', 16 December 2019, <https://www.nato.int/cps/en/natohq/news_172100.htm>, accessed 19 January 2020.

NATO Leaders' Meeting in 2019,[24] nor aimless – far from it. However, there is no room for complacency: it is imperative that NATO act on its recognition of the south as a core focus area. NATO must proactively strengthen both non-military and military activities. At the strategic-political level, NATO must enhance its diplomatic and public diplomacy initiatives regarding Turkey, with particular reference to its relations with Greece and Cyprus, and its bilateral relations with the US. Discussions of Libya must similarly gain prevalence within NATO, with a focus on aligning member states' policies and their actions on the ground to the extent possible. These steps would also open up the possibility of a more comprehensive approach to containing Russian military, political and intelligence activities across the northern, eastern and southern regions. With regard to military activity, NATO should build on the decision made at the 2016 Summit to expand non-Article 5 naval operations by extending these operations across the Mediterranean and continuing to build its presence in the Black Sea.

At the organisational level, NATO should broaden the vision for the south beyond the NSD − S Hub by creating additional projects with smaller mandates on particular issues or regions across the Alliance and by creating programme funding for local NGOs and institutions in the south to engage with NATO concerns. It should also recruit more civilian personnel with regional and programme management expertise, as this would provide a way to physically anchor the organisation in the south. NATO might also consider altering its official second-language requirement to include languages of countries in the southern region in order to improve its cultural diversity and expand its potential recruitment pool. All these steps would require the Alliance to proactively integrate more civilian experts and to challenge the gap that persists between civilian and military expertise.

## Conclusion

The snapshot provided in this chapter leads to one overarching conclusion: while NATO might have been forgiven in the past for not seeing the south as a priority, the current operating environment requires more than diplomatic gestures in statements and limited initiatives that linger, with inadequate resourcing, in the furthest reaches of NATO's orbit. From deployments to exercises to funding projects, outreach and communication programmes, NATO must act on the recognition that the south is a strategic priority if it is to avoid ending up with weakened collective deterrence, strained political relations and reduced room for manoeuvre at the same time as adversaries are increasing their efforts to exploit its weaknesses.

---

[24] *The Economist*, 'Emmanuel Macron Warns Europe: NATO is Becoming Obsolete', 7 November 2019.

# VII. NATO'S MARITIME DOMAIN

## KEITH BLOUNT AND JAMES HENRY BERGERON

We have now entered the third decade of the 21$^{st}$ century, a period which has witnessed waves of terrorism, the resurgence of Russia and the rise of China as central security challenges. Throughout this period, NATO has been on a continuous journey to adapt in order to retain its credibility and relevance as the world's premier multinational security institution in the West and, indeed, in the world.

The maritime domain has been an intrinsic part of this story and has again become a principal stage for strategic competition. The geography of this dynamic is new and strongly focused on the seas and the littorals. In the Cold War, we looked east to the Fulda Gap as the flashpoint of conflict with the Soviet Union. Today, however, Russian strategy is to project power and focus efforts almost everywhere except the plains of central Europe, but particularly at sea. Further afield, China has emerged as a great naval power that is increasingly present in NATO waters.

Since the creation of the NATO Response Force in 2002, the Alliance has been bolstering its ability to rapidly and credibly respond in a crisis.[1] There is now a growing appreciation that to credibly deter aggression, NATO must demonstrate its ability to act simultaneously across land, sea, air, space and cyberspace. That means dealing not only with concurrent challenges in multiple regions, but also with cyber and space warfare, disinformation and fake news. The strategic seas of the Alliance are a connective tissue between all these domains, cementing the distinctive role of maritime power in both deterrence and defence. Delivering this for

---

[1] The principal NATO military response mechanism is the NATO Response Force, backed by Follow-On Forces. Since 2016, this has been augmented by rotational Enhanced Forward Presence battlegroups in the Baltic states and Poland. See NATO, 'NATO Response Force', <https://www.nato.int/cps/en/natolive/topics_49755.htm>, accessed 7 February 2020.

NATO is the task of the Allied Maritime Command (MARCOM). This chapter considers current and prospective challenges in the maritime domain, assesses NATO's current deterrence and defence posture at sea and suggests steps that it might take to sustain its operational superiority.

## The Russian Naval Challenge

The Russian Federation navy has improved considerably over the last 20 years. The recently constructed Russian light fleet of destroyers, frigates, corvettes and patrol boats armed with Kalibr long-range land-attack cruise missiles has changed the character of war at sea for the Alliance. Russia has similar sea-attack missiles that can threaten warships and merchant vessels from hundreds of miles away. Matching this new offensive capability are well-established air-defence systems such as the S-400 and coastal-defence batteries such as the Bastion. All of this leverages an asymmetry of cost-effective but relatively inexpensive systems and platforms. Russia's fleet is small, swift and not particularly sustainable, but nonetheless capable of hitting land and sea targets from stand-off ranges.

As important as the capabilities is the asymmetric strategy they support. Russian strategic thinking increasingly focuses on 'local wars' – short conflicts of which only a few weeks might involve 'high-end' warfighting; the objectives are limited and not existential for an adversary.[2] This strategy involves giving minimum notice, employing deception tactics and pushing Russia's military posture to the brink of armed attack, raising the political costs of Allied response to force a resolution on Russian terms; or failing that, executing a high-intensity, short-duration offensive to force the Alliance to back down.

A critical and new element in this strategy is electronic warfare, designed to degrade the enemy's weapons and systems. Russia's use of electronic spectrum jamming and manipulation, GPS disruption and false navigational readings is becoming common, as is the ability to interfere with undersea fibre-optic cables and pipelines.[3] Merely a credible threat to do these things gives an adversary a deterrent advantage. Cyber

---

[2] Michael Kofman, 'The Moscow School of Hard Knocks: Key Pillars of Russian Strategy', *War on the Rocks*, 21 November 2019, <https://warontherocks.com/2019/11/the-moscow-school-of-hard-knocks-key-pillars-of-russian-strategy-2/>, accessed 20 January 2020.
[3] Jim Edwards, 'The Russians are Screwing with the GPS System to Send Bogus Navigation Data to Thousands of Ships', *Business Insider*, 14 April 2019. On potential interference with underwater cables, see Cyber Security Intelligence, 'US Accuses Russia of Interfering with Undersea Cables', 25 June 2018, <https://www.cybersecurityintelligence.com/blog/us-accuses-russia-of-interfering-with-undersea-cables-3482.html>, accessed 31 January 2020.

weapons offer the least expensive method of attack and are largely deniable – thus constituting the perfect hybrid weapon. Cyber security is a major security concern of the world shipping community today, and that threat has an impact on navies as well, since too often ships communicate on insecure circuits.[4]

An important factor in Russia's overall maritime capability is the speed with which its naval forces can act. Enjoying unity of command, indigenous equipment, aligned tactics, training and procedures, and a common culture, the Russian fleet can set sail quickly and with little notice. Russia's strategy counts on that cohesion and agility being superior in the early phase of conflict to the Alliance's ability to integrate operations among more than a dozen major navies.

There is an additional factor to consider: an ironic outcome of effective conventional and nuclear deterrence – which NATO arguably presents in any 'long-war' scenario – is to drive a peer competitor to a hybrid or 'grey-zone' strategy. Examples include the disruption of freedom of navigation in the Black Sea, GPS jamming in the Eastern Mediterranean and the seizure of Ukrainian patrol boats in the Kerch Strait in 2018.[5] This creates the operational dilemma of sub-threshold activity and how to defend against it.

## The Atlantic Nexus

The North Atlantic, Arctic and Baltic regions form a strategic 'Atlantic Nexus'. As recently demonstrated in the Russian navy's 2019 Exercise *Ocean Shield*, assets from both the Northern and Baltic fleets can be redirected to concentrate force across this area.[6] The character of the Atlantic Nexus has changed remarkably since the Cold War. Then, as now, NATO's critical challenge in the North Atlantic is to protect the sea lines of communication and transatlantic resupply in a conflict by keeping Russian forces contained above the Norwegian Sea. But the Arctic, once valuable only as the cover for Russia's nuclear-powered, ballistic missile-carrying submarine force, is now a contested civil and economic space. Furthermore, the Baltic dilemma is inverted from its Cold War manifestation: then NATO's strategy was to keep the Soviet Navy from

---

[4] See Chris Baraniuk, 'How Hackers are Targeting the Shipping Industry', *BBC News*, 18 August 2017.
[5] See Holly Ellyatt, 'Ukraine Guilty of Dangerous "Provocations", Russia Says After it Seizes Ships', *CNBC*, 27 November 2018, <https://www.cnbc.com/2018/11/27/ukraine-guilty-of-dangerous-provocations-russia-says-after-it-seizes-ships.html>, accessed 31 January 2020.
[6] See Tim Ripley, 'Russia Kicks off Baltic Naval Exercise', *Jane's*, <https://www.janes.com/article/90253/russia-kicks-off-baltic-naval-exercise>, accessed 31 January 2020.

breaking out into the Atlantic through the Danish Straits or the Kattegat; today the strategy focuses on ensuring that NATO maritime forces can break in to help defend its Baltic Allies.

The Atlantic Nexus disappeared from NATO's agenda after the demise of the Soviet Union, and until recently few were adept in the art of transatlantic maritime resupply. Since 2014, NATO has recognised the challenge and in 2018 empowered MARCOM as the 360-degree Maritime Theatre Component Command while establishing Joint Force Command Norfolk with the mandate to secure Atlantic sea lines of communication.[7] The US Second Fleet has been stood up again with a strong Arctic and North Atlantic focus. The German navy is developing a Baltic-facing maritime headquarters at Rostock that may in the future take on coordination and (during a conflict) command roles for Allied naval forces in the Baltic.[8]

At the heart of this Atlantic challenge is the submarine threat. Recent years have seen an explosion in studies on the need to protect transatlantic sea lines of communication against the Russian submarine force as part of NATO's credible deterrent posture.[9] These have been paralleled by conversations and planning inside the Alliance. Unsurprisingly, reinvigorating NATO's anti-submarine warfare (ASW) capability is a high priority for NATO and MARCOM. More than any other form of naval warfare, ASW operations must battle the elements as much as an adversary. The sheer size of the oceans presents difficulties for both attacker and defender, not least as the result of the reduced fleets of surface ships, submarines and maritime patrol aircraft on all sides. New technology also portends a change in both the lethality of submarines and the possibility of detecting them by non-acoustic means.[10]

---

[7] See NATO, 'Secretary General Previews Meeting of NATO Defence Ministers', 6 June 2018, <https://www.nato.int/cps/en/natohq/news_155283.htm>, accessed 20 January 2020.
[8] Magnus Nordenman, 'Back to the North: The Future of the German Navy in the New European Security Environment', Center for Security Studies, *ETHzürich*, 25 April 2017, <https://css.ethz.ch/en/services/digital-library/articles/article.html/0b853899-0ca6-49f6-93d2-baaf99f273df/pdf>, accessed 20 January 2020.
[9] See Kathleen H Hicks et al., *Undersea Warfare in Northern Europe* (New York, NY: Center for Strategic and International Studies/Rowman and Littlefield, 2016); Magnus Nordenman, 'Back to the Gap: The Re-Emerging Maritime Contest in the North Atlantic', *RUSI Journal* (Vol. 162, No. 1, 2017), pp. 24–30; Rowan Allport, 'Fire and Ice: A New Maritime Strategy for NATO's Northern Flank', Human Security Centre, December 2018; Magnus Nordenman, *The New Battle for the Atlantic: Emerging Naval Competition with Russia in the Far North* (Annapolis, MD: Naval Institute Press, 2019).
[10] See David Hambling, 'China's Quantum Submarine Detector Could Seal South China Sea', *New Scientist*, 22 August 2017, <https://www.newscientist.com/article/2144721-

But there is a second dilemma in relation to the Atlantic Nexus: the peacetime impact of the Russian navy's 'Kalibrisation' coupled with these forces' presence in the Eastern Atlantic and the Mediterranean. This leaves the western flank of Europe potentially vulnerable to missile attack from the sea. Although of limited use in a protracted and major conflict, such naval forces fit well with a hybrid strategy based on a short-war model that seeks to intimidate the Alliance into backing down in a crisis. Effective deterrence in this scenario depends on NATO's ability to counter that threat and assure Allies through its credible naval capability and persistent presence when needed, before crisis occurs. That requires a fully resourced Standing Naval Force and close coordination among Allied forces operating under national command.

*Norway and Iceland*

The defence of Norway and Iceland presents unusual joint challenges that have maritime power at their core. Both countries occupy critical strategic space in the Atlantic Nexus. Carrier strike and amphibious power projection provide the main, although by no means exclusive, sword and shield in contesting the North Atlantic in a conflict. New questions abound: how can NATO best use aircraft carriers in the North Atlantic given today's technologies? How does the Kalibrisation of the Russian fleet alter both Russian and NATO strategy? Arguably, Norway and Iceland are even more valuable to the Alliance deterrent posture today than during the Cold War, given NATO's need to reinforce its ability to operate in contested northern waters against credible adversary forces.

*The Baltic Sea*

NATO's objectives in the Baltic Sea are clear and indeed are the same objectives it has everywhere: to deter conflict and, if necessary, to defeat aggression. NATO must find ways to perform four critical tasks to prevail in the Baltic: counter Russia's potential for destabilising hybrid tactics and the clever use of 'lawfare'; enable NATO naval forces to demonstrate the capability to break into the Baltic past the Danish Straits; operate with acceptable risk inside an anti-access/area denial (A2/AD) space or neutralise that capability; and enjoy effective support and resupply from regional ports.[11] For amphibious forces, this includes overcoming A2 strategies to deploy forces ashore. It must be emphasised that these tasks

---

chinas-quantum-submarine-detector-could-seal-south-china-sea/#ixzz69zW3p7KB>, accessed 20 January 2020.

[11] See Heinrich Lange et al., *To the Seas Again: Maritime Defence and Deterrence in the Baltic Region* (Tallinn: International Centre for Defence and Security, 2019).

require joint and multidomain responses; the navies of individual NATO members cannot execute all these operations alone. Furthermore, as recently noted by the commandant of the US Marine Corps, General David H Berger, amphibious power ashore may play a key role in easing the pressure on deployed naval assets.[12]

Since 2016, NATO and individual Allies have bolstered their Baltic presence and improved their responsiveness to ensure that even a bloodless fait accompli attack on any part of the Alliance will prompt an effective NATO response. NATO has also placed a strong focus on improving defence capabilities and joint integration of maritime forces with Enhanced Forward Presence battlegroups as well as NATO Multinational Corps Northeast. These actions are all matched by efforts at the political and senior military levels to engage Russian leadership in order to avoid misperception while signalling NATO's resolve to ensure the freedom and security of its members.

The regional dimension of Baltic defence ought to be highlighted, given the strategic risk to immediate reinforcement posed by possible Russian operations through the Danish Straits and by Russian A2/AD systems. There is a growing and recognised need for Baltic region navies to exercise local sea denial, keep the sea lanes open from the threat of mines and maintain situational awareness that they can in turn share with Allies. Poland's 2017 maritime security strategy highlights the country's objective to provide greater support for Alliance security in the Baltic Sea.[13] The Estonian, Latvian and Lithuanian navies are similarly proactively considering the roles they can play in the future, while the German navy's headquarters in Rostock will play an important role. NATO's Swedish and Finnish partners are also key stakeholders in the security of the region.

*The Arctic and the High North*
Finally, NATO has more than a theoretical interest in the High North, since its Treaty Area of Responsibility for Collective Defence includes the territories, ships and aircraft of Allies in the North Atlantic above the Tropic of Cancer. That area has always been defined as reaching to the North Pole. Five of the eight Arctic Council members and four of five littoral states are NATO Allies.

---

[12] US Marine Corps, Department of the Navy, 'Commandant's Planning Guidance', 2019, <https://www.hqmc.marines.mil/Portals/142/Docs/%2038th%20Commandant%27s%20Planning%20Guidance_2019.pdf?ver=2019-07-16-200152-700>, accessed 20 January 2020.
[13] Polish National Security Bureau, 'Poland's Strategic Concept for Maritime Security', 2017, <https://en.bbn.gov.pl/ftp/dok/SKBMRPENG.pdf>, accessed 20 January 2020.

The Arctic was a contested undersea space in the Cold War and Russia still maintains its seaborne deterrent there. But new dynamics have emerged as a result of climate change and its effect on the Northern Sea Route, Russia's strongly asserted claims over Arctic transits, the risk of environmental damage and the growing influence of China. The Arctic connects naval force deployments between several regions. As transit opens up, that connection will grow, opening quick inter-fleet transit between the Atlantic and the Pacific to all major naval powers. That will present a challenge in ensuring freedom of the seas – for all – and maintaining a rules-based international order.

## The Mediterranean Nexus
A strategic link also exists among the Atlantic approaches to the Mediterranean through the Pillars of Hercules, the Mediterranean itself with its Ionian and Aegean Seas, and the almost-enclosed Black Sea. The operational dilemma in the Mediterranean Nexus stems from the complex mix of conventional military and insurgent or terrorist threats operating in or emanating from this area.

### The Eastern Mediterranean
The Eastern Mediterranean is strongly affected by the war in Syria, migration tensions and the Russian naval presence. It has been said that if the North Atlantic is the Russian navy's highway, the Eastern Mediterranean is its playground and tactical laboratory. Electronic jamming and spoofing have increased substantially in the region.[14] As a result, the Eastern Mediterranean is a principal site of great power competition and deterrence management.

In spring 2016, NATO directed MARCOM to stand up a maritime surveillance activity in the Aegean to help the Greek and Turkish coast guards and the European Border and Coast Guard Agency (Frontex) tackle illegal migrant trafficking.[15] MARCOM had Standing NATO Maritime Group 2 (SNMG2) on station in the area within two days – a good example of the rapid response that the Standing Groups can provide. Soon after NATO launched this effort, migration rates across the Aegean collapsed, driven by the EU–Turkey agreement and the closing of borders

[14] Edwards, 'The Russians are Screwing with the GPS System to Send Bogus Navigation Data to Thousands of Ships'; Cyber Security Intelligence, 'US Accuses Russia of Interfering with Undersea Cables'.
[15] See NATO, 'NATO Defence Ministers Agree on NATO Support to Assist with the Refugee and Migrant Crisis', 11 February 2016, <https://www.nato.int/cps/en/natohq/news_127981.htm>, accessed 20 January 2020.

in southeast Europe. But the SNMG2 deployment played its part as an element in the complex chemistry that has significantly reduced the massive flows to the islands.

In the Central Mediterranean, the major challenges are political instability and the transnational criminal networks that help sustain it. The Libyan conflict has continued into 2020, partly fuelled by external financing and proxy forces that threaten to regionalise the conflict. As a part of this, arms trafficking and illegal fuel transfers have spread to the maritime domain.[16]

NATO engages in many initiatives to counter terror and regional instability, and one of its instruments is Operation *Sea Guardian* (OSG), established in 2016. Building on the experience of Operation *Active Endeavour*, OSG was granted a much wider mandate to address maritime security challenges, using separately resourced forces so that NATO's Standing Naval Forces can remain focused on day-to-day deterrence, training and other activities. The mission has a more mature and geopolitically relevant approach to its objectives than *Active Endeavour*. Rather than looking for 'terrorists' in the abstract, OSG focuses on the flows of arms, fuel and contraband between North Africa, the Central Mediterranean and the Eastern Mediterranean that can fund terrorism. It is also working to understand the underlying dynamic and then be ready to act against it where possible. In this regard, OSG will also contribute to the situational awareness and capacity-training work undertaken by NATO's Strategic Direction – South Hub, which was established at Joint Force Command Naples in 2017 as a fusion centre for Mediterranean security awareness.[17]

The mission also presents excellent opportunities to deepen NATO's cooperation with the EU counter-migrant trafficking initiative called Operation *Sophia*. NATO and the EU have agreed that NATO will support *Sophia* with logistics and information, but further areas of cooperation are being discussed in Brussels.[18] The two headquarters are in regular contact and the collaboration is mutually beneficial.

---

[16] See *Reuters*, 'Several Countries have Breached Arms Embargo Agreed at Libya Summit – U.N.', 25 January 2020, <https://uk.reuters.com/article/uk-libya-security/several-countries-have-breached-arms-embargo-agreed-at-libya-summit-u-n-idUKKBN1ZO0SQ>, accessed 31 January 2020.

[17] See NATO, 'NSD-S Hub Mission', <https://thesouthernhub.org/about-us/mission>, accessed 20 January 2020; Colin Wall, 'NATO's New Window to the South', *Atlantic Council*, 15 August 2018, <https://www.atlanticcouncil.org/blogs/new-atlanticist/nato-s-new-window-to-the-south/>, accessed 20 January 2020.

[18] Stefano Marcuzzi, 'NATO-EU Maritime Cooperation: For What Strategic Effect?', *NDC Policy Brief Series* (No. 7-18, 2019), <http://www.ndc.nato.int/news/news.php?icode=1251>, accessed 20 January 2020.

*The Black Sea*

The Black Sea presents special challenges to Alliance security. Among all of NATO's strategic bodies of water, it has seen the greatest change in Russian naval posture over the past decade. Once rusting and moribund, Russia's Black Sea fleet is now one of the most agile and effective in the Russian navy and the most powerful naval force in the region. Russia's recent efforts to claim the Black Sea as a proprietary space include attacks on Ukrainian vessels in the Sea of Azov, harassment of Allied naval forces and the establishment of overly broad navigational warning areas.[19] Such behaviour risks an inadvertent and unnecessary clash.

The operational dilemma results from the Black Sea's almost enclosed nature and the limits on the numbers of ships, tonnage and length of stay of non-regional navies in peacetime imposed by the Montreux Convention. Within those limits, NATO has acted to expand its maritime presence and enhance regional capabilities. In 2018, NATO tripled the sea days of its Standing Naval Forces, and the forces participated in several exercises designed to improve skills – including in ASW – and help Allies to operate as an integrated force.

## China

NATO's traditional competitor has always been Russia, but the Alliance cannot ignore the rise of China's naval service. While China is still predominantly a regionally focused maritime power, confronting many unresolved geopolitical challenges in its immediate geographic area, military adventurism 'out of area' nevertheless appears to mirror its global policy of economic expansion. The Chinese navy's reach includes recent exercises with Russia's navy in South Africa, a well-funded base in Djibouti and, in the High North, the goal of a stakeholder role as a 'near Arctic nation'.[20] With two aircraft carriers at sea and more under construction, China has a declared objective of full military development by 2035 with the aim of 'resolving the Taiwan problem' by 2048.[21] It should therefore come as no surprise that the recent NATO Leaders'

[19] Megan Eckstein, 'Foggo: U.S., NATO Naval Forces Pushing Back Against Russian Harassment', US Naval Institute, 9 September 2018, <https://news.usni.org/2018/10/09/foggo-us-nato-naval-forces-pushing-back-russian-anti-access-behaviors>, accessed 7 February 2020.

[20] Andrew Wong, 'China: We Are a "Near-Arctic State" and We Want a "Polar Silk Road"', *CNBC*, 14 February 2018, <https://www.cnbc.com/2018/02/14/china-we-are-a-near-arctic-state-and-we-want-a-polar-silk-road.html>, accessed 31 January 2020.

[21] *Business Standard*, 'China to Build World-Class Armed Forces by 2035: Xi Jinping', 18 October 2017, <https://www.business-standard.com/article/international/china-to-

Meeting in London devoted time to consider the rise of China and the security challenges this poses.

The increasing presence of Chinese naval power in the transatlantic area raises questions regarding how NATO should respond. In June 2019, the US Department of Defense warned that China might position its ballistic missile submarines under the Arctic ice cap.[22] Russian military specialist Alexander Shirkorad has written in support of such Russian–Chinese cooperation in this regard and the Chinese navy of late has taken an interest in under-ice operations.[23] Such a move – indeed, any significant joint military posture with Russia in the Western Hemisphere – could have serious implications for NATO's maritime deterrent posture. In addition, Chinese strategic acquisitions in its Belt and Road Initiative of key maritime infrastructure in Europe might potentially impair NATO's military readiness or logistical flexibility.[24]

## Building Credible Capability into NATO's Maritime Response

In 2019, NATO adopted a new military strategy, its first for almost 50 years. Building on that strategy, NATO has undertaken implementing work that is significant in both size and scale, called 'Deterrence and Defence of the Euro-Atlantic Area'. This addresses the challenges noted above, principally through the concept of 'deterrence management'. It places new responsibilities on the Joint Force Commands to coordinate deterrence across all domains to deliver a synchronised, sophisticated and appropriate force posture.

Credible warfighting capability and coherent command and control remain the bedrock of the Alliance's deterrent posture, however much its application may be varied or nuanced. Since 2014, the Alliance has taken a number of steps to reassert its traditional superiority in the maritime domain. Changes began with the MARCOM headquarters itself, which, since 2016, has re-established itself as the principal maritime coordinating hub for NATO and has now been expanded and received a new mandate as NATO's Maritime Theatre Component Command. This role extends the function of the commander of MARCOM as NATO's Principal Maritime Advisor and involves a closer relationship with the Joint Force Commands,

build-world-class-armed-forces-by-2035-xi-jinping-117101800332_1.html>, accessed 31 January 2020.
[22] Phil Stewart and Idrees Ali, 'Pentagon Warns on Risk of Chinese Submarines in Arctic', *Reuters*, 2 May 2019.
[23] Lyle J Goldstein, 'Chinese Nuclear Armed Submarines in Russian Arctic Ports? It Could Happen', *National Interest*, 1 June 2019.
[24] Keith Johnson, 'Why is China Buying up Europe's Ports?', *Foreign Policy*, 2 February 2018.

ensuring that maritime effects are synchronised with other components in the overall management of joint deterrence.

This joint deterrent posture requires an effective maritime force under NATO control, supported by credible Allied naval assets that could quickly join in a crisis. The Standing Naval Force that MARCOM commands plays a key role in the NATO Response Force (NRF) package and the four Standing Groups of Allied ships that comprise it are NATO's first responders. When robustly manned, the Standing Groups are a potent force, more powerful than most countries could field on their own and at far less cost to each supporting navy. MARCOM typically commands 10 surface combatants and nine mine countermeasures vessels, deployed, fully certified and ready. A single navy fielding a sustainable deployed force of that size would need at least 30 surface combatants and 27 mine countermeasures vessels in its inventory.

To underpin Allied ability to operate in challenging threat environments, MARCOM and the Allied navies have focused very heavily on training. Exercises *Dynamic Mongoose* in the North Atlantic and *Dynamic Manta* in the Mediterranean have improved NATO's ASW capabilities. In 2016, MARCOM conducted a major maritime exercise, *Noble Mariner*, off the coast of Scotland, which was fused for the first time with the UK's *Unmanned Warrior* exercise to train with and against unmanned vehicles in the air, surface and subsurface environments – the first exercise at such a scale.

More broadly, NATO has leveraged multi-domain exercises such as *Joint Warrior*, *BALTOPS* and *Maritime Express* to build surface warfare and air-defence capability in support of a reinforced Allied maritime posture, as directed by the heads of state and governments at the Warsaw Summit.[25] The recent NATO Readiness Initiative (NRI) will ensure that 30 additional Allied naval assets will be ready to join the NRF within 30 days of its activation. Together, the NRF and NRI imply a naval force of between 60 and 65 naval vessels, as well as associated maritime patrol aircraft and submarines, within a 30-day response timeframe. This constitutes the bulk of ready, sustainable Euro-Atlantic Allied naval forces.

As the Maritime Theatre Component Commander for Allied Command Operations, one of MARCOM's key functions in crisis and conflict is to advise SACEUR on maritime force allocation and prioritisation among multiple joint task forces operating in different strategic seas. To coordinate this potent force in peacetime, MARCOM has recast its relationship with maritime

[25] NATO, 'Warsaw Summit Communiqué Issued by the Heads of State and Government Participating in the Meeting of the North Atlantic Council in Warsaw 8–9 July 2016', 9 July 2016, para. 48, <https://www.nato.int/cps/en/natohq/official_texts_133169.htm>, accessed 7 February 2020.

stakeholders. It has proposed a new 'Standing NATO Maritime Framework' that encourages and facilitates information exchange at speed and will allow MARCOM to be both a hub and a portal for all events at sea and for consultations on how to respond.

## Looking to the Future

The challenges described above would suggest seven areas that merit near-term efforts by the Alliance to further improve its deterrent capabilities at sea. First, navies succeed or fail as part of a multi-domain effort. NATO must foster full integration in its operations, between maritime and land-based air power, with land forces and also in links to space and cyber operations. This work is progressing rapidly.

Second, NATO could place greater emphasis on power projection. In recent years, the Alliance may have concentrated too much on countering adversary offensive systems and not enough on bolstering its own. Wars are not won nor peace maintained by playing only defence; NATO must also be able to hold potential adversary interests or manoeuvre forces at risk. Maritime NATO thus needs depth and credibility in carrier strike and amphibious power projection that are visibly integrated into joint effects. The F-35 and other fifth-generation capabilities are critical to both. NATO should also bolster the offensive strike doctrine and tactics for frigates.

Third, the Alliance needs to provide an effective counter to the Russian navy's Kalibr fleet and the threat of land attack from Russian ships at sea. After five years of tracking Russia's light, distributed fleet of Kalibr platforms and posturing forces against them, MARCOM has learned that a credible but nuanced NATO maritime presence where the Kalibr platforms are located enhances deterrence. That presence requires a fully manned, fully ready Standing Naval Force as well as parallel national deployments. NATO and Allied units must be able to assure the Alliance – and convey to a potential adversary – that NATO can manage and counter the missile threat on Day Zero of a conflict.

Fourth, NATO should strengthen efforts to deliver ASW capability in depth. MARCOM has a critical need for continuous ready access to a minimum ASW force in strategic seas such as the North Atlantic and the Mediterranean, even if that only takes the form of one effective ASW frigate with a towed array, one modern diesel submarine and a regular maritime patrol aircraft schedule. Again, a fully resourced Standing Naval Force will meet this need, but where numbers are lacking, some alternative arrangement may be required.

Fifth, NATO must leverage innovation in unmanned and autonomous systems as well as new technologies to greater effect. MARCOM fostered experimentation with autonomous underwater vehicles in *Unmanned*

*Warrior* off Scotland's coast and has pushed that agenda in every ASW exercise it could. Closer cooperation with NATO's Centre for Maritime Research and Experimentation is needed to bring the products of research and development into NATO for operational exploitation. This effort calls for further development and a regular programme; it would pay substantial dividends in the current race for technological advantage.

Sixth, the Alliance needs to continue to develop and evolve the way in which it works with Allied forces working under national command, not only to better deliver more coordinated deterrence to prevent escalation or miscalculation, but also to ensure that, should deterrence fail, NATO command and control is agile enough for the Alliance to win any short war. Any presumption by a competitor that NATO's liberal democracies and their navies will be slow to react in the transition to, or in the early phases of, conflict must be dispelled through more sophisticated exercising and other peacetime activity.

Finally, and encompassing all the other recommendations, greater investment in NATO's strategic communications dimension could bolster its maritime deterrent posture. Operationally, NATO's current deterrence challenge is to sense danger early, project forces rapidly and further remove any belief of an easy win or fait accompli from an adversary's calculus. No one can win a long war of attrition with the NATO Alliance, and potential adversaries know it; the test of deterrence today is precluding a misguided attempt to launch a short war for limited goals. NATO needs not only to have the means to make that case, but also to communicate that message effectively.

## Conclusion

Individually these improvements are important, but collectively they can be game changers in the Alliance's collective deterrent posture and readiness against traditional and emergent challenges. NATO already possesses the advantages of force and mass at sea; the capability gap to be addressed relates to joint integration, speed of response, agility in fielding critical capabilities when and where needed, re-asserting the Alliance's coordinated ability to project power and addressing a new generation of weapons and tactics. Achieving these will ensure that the maritime domain remains one in which the Alliance possesses a strategic advantage well into the 21$^{st}$ century.

# VIII. MAINTAINING NATO'S TECHNOLOGICAL EDGE

## TIM SWEIJS AND FRANS OSINGA

The character of modern armed conflict is changing rapidly. Major powers have integrated new generations of military hardware as well as an assortment of enabling technologies into their force postures and warfighting strategies. Violent non-state actors have also significantly enhanced their power projection capabilities. These developments have a profound impact on the conditions underlying international stability and will change the face of battle. This chapter first outlines current and near-future (five- to 10-year) developments in cyber, artificial intelligence (AI), unmanned systems and space, and assesses their consequences for international security and stability. It then examines the implications for NATO, arguing that the Alliance risks losing its military-technological edge vis-à-vis near-peer competitors if it does not increase its investments and efforts in these areas. It also lays out the strategic, moral and practical challenges that these new technologies pose, in particular for European member states, and offers four recommendations for NATO action going forward.

## Military-Technological Trends and their Military-Strategic Implications
### Cyber
Cyberspace has now been established as another warfighting domain and strategists have moved beyond debating whether or not cyber war will take place.[1] The past decade saw countries develop cyber weapons and doctrines and establish cyber commands to execute operations in the

---

[1] Thomas Rid, 'Cyber War Will Not Take Place', *Journal of Strategic Studies* (Vol. 35, No. 1, 2012), pp. 5–32.

cyber domain. This early phase in cyber warfare also featured the first deployment of cyber instruments in the context of military operations alongside continuous lower-level cyber skirmishes, infiltrations of adversary networks, large-scale theft of critical national security technologies and sabotage of vital infrastructures.[2] In the next phase, states will continue to expand and refine their cyber arsenals and experiment with cyber operations to explore the extent to which they can achieve operationally and strategically relevant effects. Both theory and practice regarding the use and utility of cyber weapons as strategic instruments will gain more depth and breadth in continuous and close interaction with each other. If initial state military cyber forays could be characterised, in one of Deng Xiaoping's unforgettable phrases, as 'crossing the river by feeling the stones', the next few years are likely to involve greater experimentation, followed, eventually, by some degree of maturation, analogous to the way air strategy and doctrine developed in the first half of the 20th century.

The still-nascent strategic knowledge base concerning how military cyber weapons can be created, maintained and used will inevitably expand and spread to more state and non-state actors. It will include best practices and standard procedures for how to structure 'exploit development cycles', how to compare and rate the strategic value of classes of zero-day vulnerabilities and when to best make use of them given their 'transitory nature'.[3] This will undoubtedly result in a more differentiated and mature portfolio of cyber weapons. Meanwhile, both military and political decision-makers will likely improve their understanding of the cyber domain and the potential effects of cyber weapons. This will be facilitated by the further elaboration and refinement of strategies and doctrines describing when and how cyber instruments can be deployed.

At the operational level, cyber capabilities will be critical enablers of military action. Even more than now, the conduct of future war will depend on command, control, communications, computers, intelligence, surveillance and reconnaissance (C4ISR) capabilities. Robust cyber network protection will therefore be a sine qua non for any future fighting force. Offensive military cyber capabilities will be instrumental in blinding

---

[2] Alexander Klimburg, *The Darkening Web: The War for Cyberspace* (New York, NY: Penguin Press, 2017).

[3] Lillian Ablon and Andy Bogart, *Zero Days, Thousands of Nights: The Life and Times of Zero-Day Vulnerabilities and Their Exploits* (Santa Monica, CA: RAND Corporation, 2017), pp. 65–72; Max Smeets, 'A Matter of Time: On the Transitory Nature of Cyberweapons', *Journal of Strategic Studies* (Vol. 41, No. 1–2, 2018), pp. 6–32.

the enemy by eliminating adversarial C4ISR structures. At the tactical level, power will be partially pushed to the edge, with capabilities trickling down to tactical cyber units that will have access to reach-back facilities. This will occur in the context of the further fusion of the cyber and electromagnetic spheres, leading to the formation of cyber and electromagnetic activities (CEMA) teams.

Meanwhile, continued progress in AI will further drive the automation of both offensive and defensive cyber tasks (for example, identifying critical vulnerabilities in adversary systems or patching security gaps). This will expedite the development of 'cyber centaur' squads consisting of smart cyber programmers working in close synergy with even smarter algorithms, with the latter performing most of the complex work. Despite Google's recent claim that it has attained the 'quantum supremacy' milestone, the level of progress in quantum computing is not expected to make encryption obsolete and usher in a world of full transparency during the next decade.[4]

Over the next five years, the arrival of 5G networks will bring about the Internet of Everything, multiplying opportunities to create chaos and wreak havoc on our societies. This will facilitate two parallel developments, both of which have already started. First, it will drive the nationalisation of control over critical infrastructures and the subsequent fragmentation of the global internet. Second, it will motivate state and non-state actors to further embrace offensive cyber doctrines so that they can significantly threaten not just the military capabilities of their opponents but, and potentially more effectively from a strategic perspective, their entire societies through attacks on critical infrastructures. The exploitation of social media for the targeted distribution of disinformation will undermine societal trust in Western democratic states. Russia's intrusions into Ukrainian and US critical national infrastructures, as well as the centrality of concepts such as persistent engagement in 'grey space' and 'red space' in recent high-level US debates on cyber operations, may in that respect be only early harbingers of what is to come.[5]

---

[4] Michael E O'Hanlon, 'Forecasting Change in Military Technology, 2020–2040', Brookings Institution, September 2018.
[5] In the US Joint Publication 3-12 on cyberspace operations, 'blue space' refers to areas in cyberspace protected by the US, 'red space' refers to cyberspace owned or controlled by an adversary and 'grey space' refers to 'all cyberspace that does not meet the description of either "blue" or "red"'. See US Department of Defense, 'Joint Publication 3-12: Cyberspace Operations', 8 June 2018, p. I-5.

*Artificial Intelligence*

AI is an all-purpose enabler that will profoundly shape the ways in which armed forces fight, similar to how the internal combustion engine and the computer changed the conduct of war in previous eras.[6] The past decade saw considerable progress in deep learning and neural networking, commonly captured under the rubric of AI. During this period, machine-learning applications revolutionised a wide range of activities, from Wall Street trading (with algorithms executing over 40% of the trades) and advertising (micro-profiling and behavioural targeting), to health sciences (cancer screening). In the past two years, major military powers, in particular the US and China, have expanded their investments, with Russia, Israel, France and the UK following at a distance. Things are moving fast now: military powers publish AI strategies and establish well-funded AI centres at the heart of military institutions. Countries actively pursue civil–military fusion; in particular, China's People's Liberation Army (PLA) seeks to harness and exploit private and civil innovation through institutionalised cooperation. Current AI applications include early warning (predictive modelling), intelligence analysis (signal detection), battlespace and course-of-action analysis, target acquisition and recognition, swarming manoeuvre techniques, and command and control (C2) and (semi-)autonomous decision-making. In this context, the Chinese speak of 'intelligentized warfare', with reference to the US notion of informatised war of the 1990s when the Second Offset Strategy of the 1970s started bearing fruit.[7]

A dystopian future in which machines are not only involved in the conduct of operations but also make the decisions – which would, in effect, change the nature of war – is still a long way off.[8] The character of war will change, however, as a result of the progressive integration of AI in the modus operandi of armed forces over the course of the 2020s. Incremental improvements to military capabilities will likely ensue after a period of trial and error, and will likely also lead to benefits that include greater safety of combatants and non-combatants. A fundamental concern, however, relates to whether the successful integration and exploitation of future generations of AI will yield a quantum capability leap that will then

---

[6]  Michael C Horowitz, 'Artificial Intelligence, International Competition, and the Balance of Power', *Texas National Security Review* (Vol. 1, No. 3, May 2018), pp. 36–57.
[7]  Elsa B Kania, 'Battlefield Singularity: Artificial Intelligence, Military Revolution, and China's Future Military Power', Center for a New American Security, 28 November 2017, p. 12.
[8]  F G Hoffman, 'Will War's Nature Change in the Seventh Military Revolution?', *Parameters* (Vol. 47, No. 4, Winter 2017–18), pp. 19–31.

dramatically upset the military balance of power. Such punctuated progress may translate into first-past-the-post advantages for early adopters. Historical military parallels exist: in the past, Western powers attained a decisive military edge that lasted several centuries when they first exploited the gunpowder revolution and then unleashed the power of the Industrial Revolution in the service of military objectives. The exact form military superiority will take in the 'age of AI' is not yet clear, but military strategists on all sides are obviously hastening to envision and engineer the force of the future. Likely consequences in this time period associated with military AI applications include the cumulative acceleration of the OODA (observe, orient, decide, act) loop, the partial removal of humans from some aspects of this loop and the advent of 'hyperwar' through the employment of AI-equipped autonomous weapon systems.[9]

*Unmanned Systems*
Closely related to progress in computing power and smarter algorithms is the proliferation of unmanned platforms in the land, sea and air domains. Over 150 types of military aerial drones are in production in nearly 50 states, more than 100 states deploy drones for military purposes and at least 36 states possess, or are in the process of acquiring, armed drones.[10] At present, these drones are used primarily for C4ISR and strike. In recent years, Western powers, relying on air superiority, exploited their lead in military drone capabilities to wage a form of remote warfare: they targeted insurgent and terrorist groups, and in January 2020 even a key Iranian general, while themselves remaining seemingly invulnerable to counter-strike.[11] But the proliferation of drones will certainly put this presumed invulnerability under pressure. Due to low costs and easy availability, both state and non-state actors are obtaining and employing drones. A September 2019 article in the *New York Times*, headlined 'Boko Haram is Back. With Better Drones', captures a much wider trend prevailing in battle theatres around the globe. The Islamic State of Iraq and Syria (ISIS) has carried out attacks against Syrian civilians and Russian bases, Hizbullah has deployed them in Syria and Venezuelan opposition forces

---

[9] Paul Scharre, *Army of None: Autonomous Weapons and the Future of War*, first edition (New York, NY: W W Norton & Company, 2018).

[10] Center for a New American Security, 'Proliferated Drones: The Drone Database', <http://drones.cnas.org/drones/>, accessed 5 November 2019; New America, 'Who Has What: Countries with Armed Drones', <https://www.newamerica.org/in-depth/world-of-drones/3-who-has-what-countries-armed-drones/>, accessed 5 November 2019.

[11] Andreas Krieg and Jean-Marc Rickli, 'Surrogate Warfare: The Art of War in the 21st Century?', *Defence Studies* (Vol. 18, No. 2, 2018), pp. 113–30.

used a drone in an attempt to assassinate President Nicolás Maduro. Libyan armed groups also employed Chinese- and Turkish-manufactured drones in the ongoing civil war in summer 2019.

Progress in unmanned land and maritime vehicles has lagged somewhat behind advances in aerial platforms, but Russia, which aspires to make 30% of its land systems robotic by 2025, has already tested the Uran-9 tank in Syria. In 2018, President Vladimir Putin announced that Russia was developing the autonomous, intercontinental-range, nuclear-powered unmanned underwater vehicle (UUV), Poseidon, to carry out nuclear attacks. China displayed a revolutionary UUV alongside an air-launched supersonic drone at its 70th National Parade on 1 October 2019 and has launched an expansive programme involving the domestic production of a variety of unmanned systems for land and naval warfare.[12] As yet another sign of China's rise, it recently overtook the US as the world's foremost exporter of drones.

Trends in this sphere point towards the further proliferation of unmanned systems featuring miniaturisation and far greater endurance. Such systems will further fuel the ongoing expansion of violence and contribute to levelling the playing field between technologically advanced and less advanced actors. As T X Hammes observes, 'the proliferation of many small and smart weapons may simply overwhelm a few exceptionally capable and complex systems'.[13]

*Space*

Space assets are increasingly central to the functioning of globally networked societies. Satellite launch capabilities are proliferating, while the cost of satellites is decreasing. Fourteen states can now launch their own satellites and more than 80 states possess space-based assets, while numerous commercial providers offer services from space to anyone who can afford them.[14] Space-based assets are also increasingly critical enablers of current and future military operations, with most CS4IR functions depending on them. Major military powers without space-based assets are in essence deaf, blind and mute, and indeed paralysed.

---

[12] Vincent Boulanin and Maaike Verbruggen, 'Mapping the Development of Autonomy in Weapon Systems', SIPRI, November 2017, pp. 102–03; Office of the US Secretary of Defense, 'Annual Report to Congress: Military and Security Developments Involving the People's Republic of China 2019', May 2019.

[13] T X Hammes, 'Technologies Converge and Power Diffuses: The Evolution of Small, Smart, and Cheap Weapons', Cato Institute, Policy Analysis No. 786, 27 January 2016.

[14] Linda Dawson, *War in Space: The Science and Technology Behind Our Next Theater of Conflict* (New York, NY: Springer International Publishing, 2018), p. 13.

Intelligence, communication, precision weapons and logistics all depend on properly functioning space systems.

Not surprisingly, space is increasingly regarded as a military domain. Space is now starting to be weaponised, the terms of the 1967 Outer Space Treaty notwithstanding. In March 2019, India became the fourth country to demonstrate a direct-ascent anti-satellite (ASAT) capability in a live test, following the US, Russia and China, which first did so in 2007. These tests are emblematic of a more pervasive trend. The US, under President Donald Trump, re-established a Space Command in 2019 as a precursor to an eventual Space Force. In China, the Strategic Support Force, established in 2015, has an important role in further developing the PLA's space warfare capabilities. Russia, building on the vast infrastructure established during Soviet times, remains an important space power.

In strictly military terms, Europe's space powers lag behind China, Russia and the US, which are currently recalibrating their military space postures and are actively investing not only in greater numbers of satellites, but also in stronger protection of those systems, better encrypted download and upload datalinks, and further development of ASAT missile systems, satellite jammers and directed energy weapons.[15] China has embarked on a manned programme seeking to establish a research station on the Moon in the mid-2020s and to post humans there for extended periods in the 2030s.[16] The US also intends to return to the Moon; the first unmanned mission to transport cargo is planned for 2021, to be followed by a manned mission in 2024.[17]

Meanwhile, billionaires Elon Musk, Jeff Bezos and Richard Branson have each launched their own space corporations, based on grand visions of space exploration, exploitation and colonisation. At the same time, the US government is redrafting its rules and regulations, no longer designating space as a 'global commons' but clearly pursuing the objective to 'unshackle business activity in space'.[18] If history is any guide, attempts to establish control over economic resources will likely be accompanied by the deployment of military power to enforce and

---

[15] US Defense Intelligence Agency, 'Challenges to Security in Space', January 2019, pp. 23–28; National Air and Space Intelligence Center, 'Competing in Space', December 2018.

[16] Steven Lee Myers and Zoe Mou, '"New Chapter" in Space Exploration as China Reaches Far Side of the Moon', *New York Times*, 2 January 2019.

[17] Kenneth Chang, 'Why Everyone Wants to Go Back to the Moon', *New York Times*, 12 July 2019.

[18] Victor L Shammas and Tomas B Holen, 'One Giant Leap for Capitalistkind: Private Enterprise in Outer Space', Palgrave Communications (Vol. 5, No. 10, 2019); US Department of Commerce, 'Secretary Ross: "A Bright Future for U.S. Leadership of Space Commerce"', 21 February 2018.

guarantee that control. Space, in sum, truly constitutes a new frontier for the conduct of terrestrial and, down the line, extra-terrestrial competition and conflict.

## Implications for NATO

The literature on revolutions in military affairs (RMAs) suggests that those who manage to harness and exploit new technologies, combine them with novel operational and organisational concepts and evolve a new way of war stand to gain significantly – a sobering insight in this era of strategic competition. This is not lost on, for instance, Putin, who highlighted the impact of AI on the international order when he observed that 'artificial intelligence is the future, … whoever becomes the leader in this sphere will become the ruler of the world'.[19] Chinese leaders have expressed similar views.[20]

Whether the technological trends described above signal the advent of another RMA or merely represent incremental change remains subject to debate.[21] Regardless, the implications of the technological progress summarised here are already being made manifest and are likely to progressively materialise during the 2020s. The first attacks with swarms of drones have already taken place in Syria, Libya and Saudi Arabia, executed not by a state but by various non-state actors.

NATO members already face an assortment of challenges, including the vicious conflict dynamics in Northern Africa, the Middle East and Southwest Asia, which are not likely to disappear soon. Further, Russia's nuclear and conventional modernisation, in combination with its anti-access/area denial (A2/AD) capabilities, has cast doubt on the credibility of NATO's conventional and nuclear deterrence posture.[22] In this latter context, it has become painfully clear that the armed forces of European NATO members, in particular, have neglected the demands of joint high-intensity warfare at their own peril. For NATO, these developments therefore suggest, at a minimum, a strong imperative to not only rebuild its capabilities, but also to keep pace with rapid technological advances.

---

[19] James Vincent, 'Putin Says the Nation That Leads in AI "Will Be the Ruler of the World"', *The Verge*, 4 September 2017, <https://www.theverge.com/2017/9/4/16251226/russia-ai-putin-rule-the-world>, accessed 7 February 2020.

[20] As quoted in the read-ahead package for the NATO-Industry Forum, Berlin, 12–13 November 2018, p. 10.

[21] Kenneth Payne, *Strategy, Evolution, and War: From Apes to Artificial Intelligence* (Washington, DC: Georgetown University Press, 2018); Christian Brose, 'The New Revolution in Military Affairs: War's Sci-Fi Future', *Foreign Affairs*, May/June 2019.

[22] Elbridge Colby and Jonathan Solomon, 'Facing Russia: Conventional Defence and Deterrence in Europe', *Survival* (Vol. 57, No. 6, November 2015), pp. 21–50.

## NATO Initiatives

In recent years, NATO launched a series of initiatives to regain capabilities and expertise, with member states pledging to increase defence spending. Current capability improvement plans focus on enhancing readiness, regaining lost capabilities in artillery, tanks, transport and C2 assets; and introducing fifth-generation jet fighters in greater numbers than those ordered prior to 2014. Cyber capabilities are also receiving a boost now that cyberspace has been designated a warfighting domain. The Alliance will enhance missile defence in the next decade by fielding state-of-the-art US radar systems in various Eastern European member states. Furthermore, NATO has formulated a roadmap for research on emerging technologies such as AI, quantum computing, autonomy and hypersonic missiles. Various organisations, such as NATO's Science and Technology Organization (STO) and different centres of excellence, aim to support knowledge diffusion, create awareness and stimulate research and development. The STO conducts research on more than 250 projects across seven domains that canvass a wide spectrum of emerging technologies.[23]

European NATO member states that are also EU members have similarly agreed on a series of capability improvement initiatives. Following the 2016 EU Global Strategy, the EU launched the Coordinated Annual Review on Defence (CARD), the Permanent Structured Cooperation (PESCO) and the European Defence Fund (EDF). These initiatives focus on the range of capability targets identified in the 2018 update to the EU Capability Development Plan. The goals are to achieve a measure of strategic autonomy and to create a coherent full-spectrum force package. This force package aims to ensure air and information superiority and access to space-based systems; to support cyber response operations, naval manoeuvrability and air mobility; and finally, and more generically, to develop 'innovative technologies for enhanced future military capabilities'.[24] The US, meanwhile, has announced its determination to leverage the potential of emerging technologies in what has been labelled the 'Third Offset'. In parallel with this initiative, the US is exploring a new operational concept – 'Multi-Domain Operations' – that harnesses and exploits these new capabilities and may play the same role as the AirLand Battle concept of the 1980s.[25]

---

[23] See NATO Science and Technology Organization, 'Empowering the Alliance's Technological Edge: 2018 Highlights', March 2019, <https://www.nato.int/nato_static_fl2014/assets/pdf/pdf_2019_09/20190905_190905-STO-highlights2018.pdf>, accessed 7 February 2020.
[24] European Defence Agency, 'The EU Capability Development Priorities', 2018, pp. 6–7.
[25] David G Perkins and James M Holmes, 'Multidomain Battle: Converging Concepts Toward a Joint Solution', *Joint Force Quarterly* (Vol. 88, January 2018), pp. 54–57.

## Challenges

Despite these efforts, the developments sketched in this chapter present NATO members with an assortment of financial, ethical and military-strategic challenges. For NATO's European member states in particular, the Third Offset poses a considerable financial burden.[26] Although European member states currently spend $264 billion collectively on defence, and despite a decade of improvement initiatives, the capability shortfalls that came to light in Operation *Allied Force* in Kosovo in 1999 persist.[27] In 2012, one study concluded that without US contributions, Europe would struggle to conduct a so-called 'Small Joint Operation, Air-Heavy' – an operation comparable to Operation *Allied Force* or *Unified Protector* in Libya (2011).[28] In 2020, European armed forces remain critically dependent on the US for C4ISR and suppression of enemy air defences (SEAD) capabilities, cruise missiles, ballistic missile defence, stealth aircraft and electronic warfare assets. The same applies to creating and manning effective operational headquarters that rely on state-of-the-art C2 technology as well as expertise in operational-level planning and commanding joint operations. Estimates indicate that without the US, the defence of the Baltic states and Poland would require an additional investment by European states of about $288–357 billion.[29]

Adapting to the new geopolitical environment and implementing capability improvements for their armed forces has proven difficult for Europe's defence organisations, however, not least because of budgetary realities.[30] Defence cooperation initiatives also suffer because European defence industries remain fractured and compartmentalised along national lines, and have a diminishing ability to nationally develop and manufacture complex leading-edge military capabilities. Remedying several of the capability shortfalls – those pertaining to large and complex systems such as tanker aircraft or electronic warfare platforms – also exceeds the requirements of individual countries and calls for collective action. In addition, actually fielding the necessary new capabilities takes at least a decade.[31] Finally, while high-end weapon systems and emerging

---

[26] Luis Simón, 'The "Third" US Offset Strategy and Europe's "Anti-Access" Challenge', *Journal of Strategic Studies* (Vol. 39, No. 3, 2016), pp. 417–45.
[27] Douglas Barrie et al., 'Defending Europe: Scenario-Based Capability Requirements for NATO's European Members', International Institute for Strategic Studies, April 2019, p. 3.
[28] F Stephen Larrabee et al., *NATO and the Challenges of Austerity* (Santa Monica, CA: RAND Corporation, 2012), p. ix.
[29] Barrie et al., 'Defending Europe'.
[30] Jens Ringsmose and Sten Rynning, 'Now for the Hard Part: NATO's Strategic Adaptation to Russia', *Survival* (Vol. 59, No. 3, 2017), pp. 129–46.
[31] Barrie et al., 'Defending Europe', p. 42.

technologies claim much of the Alliance's attention, funds will also be needed for restoring more mundane capabilities such as ammunition stockpiles and transport capacity, which will enable rapid reinforcement and a sustained military campaign. Given the rather dismal European track record in actually achieving military transformation as envisioned by NATO, investments in Third Offset technologies may never actually materialise and might not produce the necessary improvements even if they did.[32]

Another challenge lies in the controversial nature of some of these technologies. While the technologies may yield many military benefits, the legality and ethics of, for instance, deploying unmanned and semi-autonomous weapon systems are hotly debated throughout society, academia, parliaments and religious circles (including the Vatican). Expert groups discuss the ethical and legal issues associated with military AI, including in the context of the UN Convention on Certain Conventional Weapons. António Guterres, former UN Secretary-General, captured prevailing concerns when he warned in 2018 that 'the prospect of machines with the discretion and power to take human life is morally repugnant'.[33] Opponents of these weapon systems allege that they will result in the 'dronification' of foreign affairs and the dehumanisation of warfare: because the use of drones reduces the need to deploy soldiers, political leaders might be more inclined to resort to force or escalation during a crisis, with war as the result. If both contestants possess such an arsenal, what happens when one of them runs out of these systems?[34] As a number of potential adversaries will certainly continue to field unmanned systems and develop military AI applications, NATO member states will need to recalibrate their capability portfolios to include defensive counter-drone capabilities and, given their increased vulnerability to drone attack, will need to reconsider which wars are worth fighting. The advent of military AI also raises military-strategic concerns, including how NATO should respond if Russia and China successfully integrate military AI and get inside Western OODA loops. NATO member states will therefore need to consider which military AI applications they want to develop and under which specific conditions they deem their use ethically acceptable.

---

[32] On the dynamics of European military innovation in the context of NATO transformation, see Terry Terriff, Frans Osinga and Theo Farrell (eds), *A Transformation Gap?: American Innovations and European Military Change* (Palo Alto, CA: Stanford University Press, 2010).

[33] António Guterres, 'Address to the General Assembly', 25 September 2018.

[34] Amitai Etzioni and Oren Etzioni, 'Pros and Cons of Autonomous Weapons Systems', *Military Review*, May 2017, pp. 71–81.

A related concern pertains to the deployment of immature AI to the battlefield, which would increase fog and friction and fuel unwanted escalatory spirals. The potential destabilising effects of the combination of new and, in some cases, untested technologies and their impact on the strategic balance of power, escalation dynamics and war presents another challenge. Emerging military space capabilities will pose a serious risk to the dynamics underlying deterrence in a multipolar world which are already under pressure due to a new generation of multiple independently targeted re-entry vehicles (MIRVs), the emergence of hypersonic (> Mach 5) missile gliders and the advent of global conventional prompt strike systems. If military powers can shut down the eyes and ears of adversaries by taking out their satellite systems, these adversaries may be unable to (fully) retaliate. This undermines credible deterrence and creates escalatory tendencies by giving parties an incentive to strike first. Ubiquitous surveillance systems (including space-based sensors) that are guided by AI and can reveal the location of nuclear missiles (even onboard submarines) increase this risk, as the accurate knowledge these systems provide might prompt pre-emptive strikes or deliberate escalation and risk-taking. Increasingly effective cyber attacks against nuclear C2 systems can likewise undermine deterrence. Hypersonic weapons (with conventional or nuclear pay loads), which can evade current state-of-the-art missile defence systems, may render C2 facilities, aircraft carriers and nuclear missile complexes vulnerable.[35] The potential unintended strategic consequences of each of the new technologies, and in particular the unpredictable effects of their deployment in combination, will certainly be topics of considerable political and societal debate within NATO's European populations that do not necessarily support increases in defence expenditures in general and increased spending on nuclear and unmanned capabilities in particular.

## Conclusions and Recommendations

The evolving geopolitical context since 2014, with the intensification of strategic interstate competition, offers a strong incentive for NATO to explore the potential of these new technologies to maintain or as necessary even regain its military edge. At the same time, NATO must

---

[35] Keir A Lieber and Daryl G Press, 'The New Era of Counterforce: Technological Change and the Future of Nuclear Deterrence', *International Security* (Vol. 41, No. 4, Spring 2017), pp. 9–49; Michael C Horowitz, 'When Speed Kills: Lethal Autonomous Weapon Systems, Deterrence and Stability', *Journal of Strategic Studies* (Vol. 42, No. 6, 2019), pp. 764–88; Jesse T Wasson and Christopher E Bluesteen, 'Taking the Archers for Granted: Emerging Threats to Nuclear Weapon Delivery Systems', *Defence Studies* (Vol. 18, No. 4, October 2018), pp. 433–53.

modernise its non-controversial military capabilities to increase its conventional deterrence in the context of inevitable budgetary constraints. Moreover, while capability improvement is crucial in the context of strategic competition, the Alliance must also maintain sufficient capacity for peace operations, security force assistance and counterterrorist activities to address persistent threats and humanitarian security risks in the 'arc of instability' surrounding Europe. Against this background, this chapter yields, at a minimum, four recommendations.

First and foremost, NATO should review its overall capability portfolio and examine how it can strike a proper balance between restoring lost capabilities and pursuing incremental modernisation on the one hand, and more punctuated (some would say disruptive) innovation on the other.

Second, NATO member states must directly address the larger strategic, ethical, legal, technological and safety issues raised by emerging technologies. These issues should not be discussed in isolation and must be considered from a variety of perspectives. It is likely that these debates will expose distinct national policy positions regarding the legitimacy and desirability of new generations and types of weapon systems and the feasibility of developing and fielding them.

Third, NATO member states will need to prioritise modernisation and investments in advanced technology research, taking into account budgetary realities, national priorities and goals, the technological sophistication of their military forces and their industrial base and their geographic proximity to (perceived) threats. Not all states will be willing to participate in a strategic competition that plays out far outside NATO territory, as the debate on the NATO Strategic Concept of 2010 already revealed.[36]

Also, while NATO is of course sensibly monitoring the developments in AI, quantum computing and so forth, most of these emerging technology trends are driven by commercial actors such as Google and Microsoft. Because the development of AI relies on factors such as the availability of data, a skilled workforce, computing power and semiconductors, disparities in how well different countries can harness these technologies and can leverage the private sector may widen in the future.[37] Some division of labour is almost inevitable between those states that host high-tech companies and related research centres and those states that have fewer such resources but are in closer proximity to potential threats. The

---

[36] See Timo Noetzel and Benjamin Schreer, 'Does a Multi-Tier NATO Matter? The Atlantic Alliance and the Process of Strategic Change', *International Affairs* (Vol. 85, No. 2, 2009), pp. 211–26.

[37] Tomáš Valášek, 'New Perspectives on Shared Security: NATO's Next 70 Years', Carnegie Europe, November 2019, p. 36.

latter will likely see themselves forced to prioritise restoration of capabilities required for repairing NATO's deterrence posture in order to address their most pressing security problems.

Moreover, European states such as Poland, Finland and Sweden may be more interested in asymmetric solutions to emerging technological threats and may choose strategies emphasising defensive capabilities and boosting societal resilience. With regard to symmetrical responses to emerging military technologies, many European NATO members will probably see their dependence on US contributions and technologies increase rather than decrease. These considerations suggest that NATO needs to develop a realistic roadmap that allows for military modernisation among NATO member states at various speeds and with varying scope, while avoiding technical, tactical and doctrinal loss of interoperability and fostering a permissive political climate among the member states that recognises the military and political merits of such an approach.

Finally, the logic of modernisation and investment in emerging technologies will benefit from the development and adoption of a coherent operational concept that undergirds NATO's conventional deterrence posture. Military innovation theory strongly suggests that innovation succeeds when it focuses on actual and pressing strategic, operational or tactical problems.[38] Tactical problems abound in Europe. For instance, air–land integration capabilities require improvement for enabling traditional close air support in a contested environment in the Baltic region. Troops, in the context of both Article 5 and crisis management operations outside of Europe, need strengthened defences against threats posed by armed helicopters, fighter bombers, (swarms of) unmanned and autonomous weapon systems and surface-to-surface missiles. Russia's A2/AD capabilities deny NATO the air superiority that it requires for C4ISR purposes and that its thin line of ground troops in Eastern Europe rely upon. This can only be remedied through the development of new defensive and offensive capabilities and concepts of operations (which might, for instance, include cyber attacks or the employment of special operations forces assets). NATO also requires short-range, mobile air defences to counter intensive barrages of cruise missiles targeting NATO airbases, C2 centres, logistical hubs and other priority targets.

These issues, in turn, are part of the operational-level challenge of restoring conventional deterrence. Deterrence during the Cold War relied

---

[38] See Williamson Murray and Allan Millett (eds), *Military Innovation in the Interwar Period* (Cambridge: Cambridge University Press, 1995), Chapters 7 and 8.

not only on nuclear weapons, tanks, submarines and fighter aircraft but also on an operational concept that tied all of these together and was designed specifically to undermine the preferred strategy of NATO's adversary. During the 1970s and 1980s, the basis for military modernisation among NATO's militaries was provided by the concept of Follow-On Forces Attack and the rediscovery of manoeuvre warfare through AirLand Battle. These concepts clearly defined roles and missions in the various domains, which in turn provided the logic for weapon system development and procurement, and for investments in promising emerging technologies. While the US is exploring the merits and implications of Multi-Domain Operations, NATO currently lacks an equivalent overarching warfighting concept. This constitutes an important weakness.

All in all, emerging technologies that are integrated into the warfighting capabilities of various non-NATO military powers, along with the greatly strengthened power projection capabilities of non-state actors, add to the political and strategic challenges NATO faces. NATO must gear up to keep pace with the rapid rate of technological change and ready itself to protect NATO members against the security threats of tomorrow. After all, the truly prudent do not seek refuge when they see danger, they prepare.[39]

---

[39] BibleGateway, 'Proverbs 22:3', <https://www.biblegateway.com/passage/?search=Proverbs+22%3A3&version=NIV>, accessed 20 January 2020.

# IX. NATO'S NUCLEAR POSTURE AND ARMS CONTROL

## CORENTIN BRUSTLEIN

Since the North Atlantic Treaty was signed and ratified by NATO's member states, the security of the Alliance has depended on the threat posed by its nuclear weapons, particularly those possessed by the US.[1] Following the shock of the Korean War and to compensate for an unfavourable conventional balance in Europe that was expected to last due to budget constraints, in 1954 the US adopted a policy of massive retaliation that emphasised 'more reliance on deterrent power and less dependence on local [conventional] defensive power'.[2] To make the threat of swift nuclear response to an attack on the US and its allies credible, Washington had already started to develop its long-range strategic forces and to deploy tactical nuclear weapons on the European continent as early as 1953. NATO's adoption of similar principles in the MC (Military Committee) 14/2 strategic concept in May 1957 opened the way to greater involvement of individual Allies in nuclear planning, command and control and operations through consultative mechanisms (particularly the Nuclear Planning Group, established in December 1966), and sharing arrangements. The US's tactical nuclear weapons of various types – artillery shells, gravity bombs, missile warheads, depth charges and so forth – forward deployed in Europe during the Cold War were all kept under US control. However, while thousands were meant to be delivered by US forces, thousands of others were deployed

---

[1]  The author would like to thank Jessica Cox and Brad Roberts for their thoughtful comments on a previous version of this chapter.
[2]  John Foster Dulles, 'The Evolution of Foreign Policy', in Philip Bobbitt, Lawrence Freedman and Gregory F Treverton (eds), *US Nuclear Strategy: A Reader* (Basingstoke: Macmillan Press, 1989), p. 124.

among Allied units and would be employed by non-US forces, all under the command of SACEUR.[3]

Since the 1960s and the Harmel report on the future tasks of the Alliance that introduced the need for the Alliance to combine deterrence and détente, NATO member states have constantly tried to balance the requirements of a credible posture of deterrence and collective defence and the need to maintain a substantive dialogue with Moscow on the ways to reduce risks and tensions in Europe.[4] Since that time, the Alliance has been a setting in which arms control policies and priorities were frequently assessed, discussed and negotiated. Still, while the contentious debates surrounding NATO's posture until 1990 often centred on nuclear weapons, the end of the Cold War opened an era during which nuclear deterrence and collective defence almost disappeared from the Alliance's agenda. As the risk of major war appeared to fade away, instability in Europe's neighbourhood and events such as the 11 September 2001 attacks prompted Allies to increasingly focus on crisis management and emerging security challenges.

The 2014 Ukraine crisis and Russia's renewed strategic assertiveness have put an end to this era by reminding Allies of the endurance of power politics and of the risk of major war, and again brought to the fore considerations related to nuclear weapons. In a context of heightened tensions and a transformed technological and operational environment, it has become necessary for Allies to rediscover that deterrence and dialogue and reinforce each other to strengthen the security of the Alliance. While some topics such as burden-sharing never disappeared entirely from NATO discussions throughout the years, current debates have focused increasingly on ways to make extended deterrence credible in the face of renewed political and operational challenges, on potential NATO responses to Russian deployment of theatre-range systems and on arms control priorities for the Alliance. This chapter provides an overview of how the Alliance of 2020 meets these renewed challenges.

---

[3] For historical overviews of NATO's nuclear policy, see Shaun R Gregory, *Nuclear Command and Control in NATO: Nuclear Weapons Operations and the Strategy of Flexible Response* (Basingstoke: Macmillan Press, 1996), pp. 15–40; J Michael Legge, *Theater Nuclear Weapons and the NATO Strategy of Flexible Response* (Santa Monica, CA: RAND Corporation, 1983), pp. 1–38; Michael O Wheeler, 'NATO Nuclear Strategy, 1949–1990', in Gustav Schmidt (ed.), *A History of NATO: The First Fifty Years*, Volume 3 (Basingstoke: Palgrave, 2001), pp. 121–39.
[4] NATO, 'The Future Tasks of the Alliance: Report of the Council – "The Harmel Report"', December 1967, <https://www.nato.int/cps/en/natohq/official_texts_26700.htm>, accessed 21 January 2020.

## The Enduring Foundations of NATO's Nuclear Policy

NATO has always been a nuclear alliance and, according to its 2010 Strategic Concept and all major NATO policy statements made since then, intends to remain so as long as nuclear weapons exist.[5] During the Cold War, NATO relied first and foremost on various types of US nuclear weapons to deter the Soviet Union and the signatory countries of the Warsaw Pact from launching a large-scale attack based on their superior conventional combat power. These included: US non-strategic nuclear weapons meant to be used by US tactical combat units in Europe or European combat units as part of nuclear sharing arrangements; US theatre-range nuclear strike systems; or, ultimately, US strategic weapons based in the continental US. Of these categories of weapon systems, only two remain active today as part of NATO's nuclear deterrence posture: US non-strategic nuclear weapons paired with European dual-capable aircraft (DCA) and US strategic forces. Since 1974, the Alliance has also acknowledged the contribution of British and French nuclear weapons to NATO's deterrence posture.[6]

As the political complement to these capability deployments, the nuclear policy of the Alliance has relied on a consultation mechanism. When NATO started to plan and exercise scenarios involving large-scale employment of nuclear weapons in Central Europe, Western European Allies voiced rising concerns about nuclear planning, command-and-control arrangements, targeting and their own ability to influence US nuclear plans that might dramatically affect their populations and territories. The Nuclear Planning Group was born out of this growing need for consultation between the country that was extending the protection offered by its nuclear weapons and the Allies benefiting from this protection. The group reflected – and still reflects – the combined need to reassure Allies and share the burden of NATO's nuclear mission among them all, while signalling collective will and still limiting the spread of nuclear weapons. All the core elements of NATO's nuclear posture – the nuclear sharing arrangements, the consultative mechanisms, and the supporting role of non-nuclear Allies – were crafted in the late 1960s, while the Nuclear Non-Proliferation Treaty (NPT) was being negotiated. Negotiators from NATO member states thus ensured that the final wording of the treaty would be compatible with the existing arrangements.[7]

---

[5] NATO, 'Active Engagement, Modern Defence', 2010.

[6] The UK has explicitly committed its nuclear forces to NATO since the early 1960s, with bombers first assigned in 1963. See Lawrence Freedman, *Britain and Nuclear Weapons* (London and Basingstoke: Royal Institute of International Affairs/ Macmillan Press, 1980), pp. 25–26.

[7] William Alberque, *The NPT and the Origins of NATO's Nuclear Sharing Arrangements*, Proliferation Papers, No. 57 (Paris: Ifri, February 2017).

After a rapid reduction in the Alliance's nuclear force posture at the end of the Cold War, the number of US non-strategic nuclear weapons forward deployed to Europe remained roughly stable at approximately 200 weapons.[8] Despite the stability that has characterised NATO's nuclear force posture since the 1990s, the Alliance has struggled to articulate a clear rationale for a deterrence and defence posture that relied in part on forward-based, non-strategic nuclear weapons, or more simply to explain how nuclear weapons help keep the Alliance secure against modern security challenges. Many factors contributed to these difficulties. First, Russia underwent a deep economic crisis that seemed to at least temporarily defang its military forces. Second, the US enjoyed overwhelming conventional superiority over all its potential adversaries, as evidenced in operations such as *Desert Storm, Allied Force, Enduring Freedom* and *Iraqi Freedom*. This led many US policymakers to believe that the country could continue reducing its reliance on nuclear weapons and still ensure a credible deterrent for both itself and its allies. Third and finally, some of these policymakers also failed to understand why Washington might ever have to threaten nuclear weapon use to protect the US and its partners, especially since nuclear weapons and nuclear power had become increasingly divisive issues in European domestic politics.

As scenarios in which NATO might have to resort to nuclear weapons appeared more remote and implausible to most Allies, the divisions between the member states supporting disarmament (or at least the removal of US weapons from Europe) and those believing in the continued importance of nuclear weapons for deterrence – including newer members – grew wider. Due to this trend and the increasing efforts NATO devoted to crisis management, counterterrorism and counterinsurgency operations, the statements and communiqués issued following NATO summits between 2000 and 2014, and even the 2010 Strategic Concept, did not convey a clear rationale for retaining nuclear weapons. Reflecting both the unease of various Allies about nuclear issues and the high priority that President Barack Obama's administration placed on reducing reliance on nuclear weapons, the 2010 Strategic Concept proclaimed that NATO's nuclear forces provided 'the supreme guarantee of the security of the Allies' but also emphasised that '[t]he circumstances in which any use of nuclear weapons might have to be contemplated are extremely remote'.[9] The 2012 Deterrence and Defence Posture Review was somewhat more specific, stating that

---

[8]   Hans M Kristensen and Matt Korda, 'Tactical Nuclear Weapons, 2019', *Bulletin of the Atomic Scientists* (Vol. 75, No. 5, 2019), pp. 257–58.
[9]   NATO, 'Active Engagement, Modern Defence', paras 17–18.

'[n]uclear weapons are a core component of NATO's overall capabilities for deterrence and defence alongside conventional and missile defence forces', but did not explicitly state the reasons why nuclear weapons still play a key role in deterrence and defence.[10]

## The Renewed Importance of Nuclear Weapons to NATO Security

The annexation of Crimea stands out as both an inflection point and a wake-up call for the Alliance. Russia's strategic resurgence, reflected in its increasingly ambitious rhetoric and uncooperative and sometimes hostile military and non-military actions, brought many within the Alliance, including the US, to reconsider their past reluctance to acknowledge the value of nuclear weapons in protecting the European status quo. Since 2014, member states have thus agreed to take various steps both to reassert the role of nuclear weapons in Alliance security and to strengthen NATO's deterrence and defence posture to ensure that it stayed credible against the full spectrum of current threats. The Wales (2014) and Warsaw (2016) Summits were both critical tests of NATO's ability to find a new consensus among Allies while crafting a coherent and firm response to the strategic challenge posed by Russia.

Allies have been debating the nature and extent of the Russian threat to the Alliance, and particularly the role played by nuclear weapons in Moscow's strategy, since 2014.[11] While describing Russia's current and future strategic policy and its force posture is beyond the scope of this chapter, four aspects of that policy merit highlighting.

First, even though Russia has not explicitly lowered its nuclear threshold in unclassified official documents, it clearly intends to exploit the shadow cast by its nuclear weapons to advance its foreign policy objectives and potentially change the territorial status quo, particularly in situations such as the Ukraine crisis in which the asymmetry of stakes between NATO and Russia seems clear. While they do not necessarily reflect a revolutionary change in Moscow's posture, thinly veiled nuclear threats, large-scale strategic exercises and announced intentions to deploy

---

[10]  NATO, 'Deterrence and Defence Posture Review', 2012, para. 8.
[11]  See Dmitry (Dima) Adamsky, *Cross-Domain Coercion: The Current Russian Art of Strategy*, Proliferation Papers, No. 54 (Paris: Ifri, November 2015); Kristin Ven Bruusgaard, 'Russian Strategic Deterrence', *Survival* (Vol. 58, No. 4, August/ September 2016), pp. 7–26; Dave Johnson, *Nuclear Weapons in Russia's Approach to Conflict* (Paris: Fondation pour la Recherche Stratégique, 2016); Olga Oliker, 'Russia's Nuclear Doctrine: What We Know, What We Don't, and What That Means', Center for Strategic and International Studies, May 2016; Bruno Tertrais, 'Russia's Nuclear Policy: Worrying for the Wrong Reasons', *Survival* (Vol. 60, No. 2, April/May 2018), pp. 33–44.

dual-capable weapon systems for coercive leverage undoubtedly reflect the higher profile of nuclear weapons in Russia's policy.[12]

Second, since the late 1990s, Moscow has both voiced its discontent with the existing arms control and confidence-building agreements and bypassed or violated most of these agreements – including the Conventional Forces Europe (CFE), Intermediate-Range Nuclear Forces (INF) and Open Skies Treaties and the Vienna Document – to increase its strategic freedom of action in its various neighbourhoods.[13]

Third, several aspects of Russia's nuclear force structure are worrying from a NATO perspective, including the imbalance between NATO and Russia in non-strategic nuclear weapons, Russia's ambitious modernisation of its strategic triad and its intention to develop new types of weapons outside the framework of the New START Treaty, as stated by President Vladimir Putin on 1 March 2018.[14]

Fourth, the new emphasis on non-nuclear strategic deterrence in Russia's 2014 military doctrine[15] serves as a reminder that the balance of conventional forces between NATO and Russia is more complex than previously assessed: Russian armed forces now possess a growing portfolio of long-range conventional strike systems intended not only as tactical capabilities, but also as strategic assets capable of deterring adversaries or compelling them to back down during a conflict.[16]

---

[12] Jacek Durkalec, *Nuclear-Backed 'Little Green Men': Nuclear Messaging in the Ukraine Crisis* (Warsaw: Polish Institute of International Affairs, 2015).

[13] Dick Zandee, 'The Future of Arms Control and Confidence-Building Regimes', Carnegie Europe, 28 November 2019, <https://carnegieeurope.eu/2019/11/28/future-of-arms-control-and-confidence-building-regimes-pub-80427>, accessed 28 January 2020.

[14] Among the five types of nuclear-capable delivery systems advertised in Putin's State of the Nation address on 1 March 2018, Russia considers that only two of the weapons proposed (the Sarmat heavy intercontinental ballistic missile (ICBM) and the Avangard hyperglide vehicle) would fall under the New START Treaty limits. The three other systems (Kinzhal air-launched ballistic missile, Burevestnik nuclear-powered cruise missile and Poseidon strategic nuclear torpedo) would be more difficult to bring within the existing categories, although a case could be made for the Kinzhal. See Vladimir Putin, 'Presidential Address to the Federal Assembly', Moscow, 1 March 2018, <http://en.kremlin.ru/events/president/news/56957>, accessed 21 January 2020; Pranay Vaddi, 'Bringing Russia's New Nuclear Weapons into New START', *Lawfare*, 13 August 2019, <https://www.lawfareblog.com/bringing-russias-new-nuclear-weapons-new-start>, accessed 21 January 2020.

[15] Russian Federation, 'The Military Doctrine of the Russian Federation', 25 December 2014, section I, para. 8m.

[16] Dave Johnson, 'Russia's Conventional Precision Strike Capabilities, Regional Crises, and Nuclear Thresholds', Livermore Papers on Global Security No. 3, February 2018, <https://cgsr.llnl.gov/content/assets/docs/Precision-Strike-Capabilities-report-v3-7.pdf>, accessed 21 January 2020.

Furthermore, the emphasis Moscow has placed during the past two decades on the development and fielding of anti-access/area denial (A2/AD) capabilities (long-range conventional strike, integrated air-defence systems, anti-ship missiles, electronic warfare and so forth) would make it more difficult and more costly for Allies to militarily support each other during a war, as both lines of communication in the Atlantic and freedom of manoeuvre in the European theatre could be held at risk by Russian capabilities in this area.

In combination, these four lasting trends have driven NATO to reassess the risk of major war and to start relearning the grammar of nuclear deterrence. As a result of these trends and the growing salience of great power competition, nuclear deterrence will remain a critical component of the Alliance's posture in the next decades. NATO's deterrence and defence posture will undoubtedly continue to rely on an 'appropriate mix' of conventional forces, missile defence and nuclear capabilities, as each plays an important role in ensuring a credible posture during the various phases of crisis and conflict. Still, in a security environment marked by geopolitical turmoil, technological change and an erosion of Western competitive military advantages in the conventional realm, the role of nuclear weapons in the Alliance's deterrence posture appears more central now than at any time since the end of the Cold War. The communiqué issued by the heads of state and governments following the 2016 Warsaw Summit both reasserted that the 'fundamental purpose' of nuclear weapons was political in nature ('to preserve peace, prevent coercion, and deter aggression') and stressed their unique value for deterrence purposes:

> The strategic forces of the Alliance, particularly those of the United States, are the supreme guarantee of the security of the Allies. The independent strategic nuclear forces of the United Kingdom and France have a deterrent role of their own and contribute to the overall security of the Alliance. These Allies' separate centres of decision-making contribute to deterrence by complicating the calculations of potential adversaries. … Nuclear weapons are unique. Any employment of nuclear weapons against NATO would fundamentally alter the nature of a conflict. The circumstances in which NATO might have to use nuclear weapons are extremely remote. If the fundamental security of any of its members were to be threatened however, NATO has the capabilities and resolve to impose costs on an adversary that would be unacceptable and far outweigh the benefits that an adversary could hope to achieve. … Missile defence can

complement the role of nuclear weapons in deterrence; it cannot substitute for them.[17]

The Alliance must recognise that major adversaries could exercise a large and growing spectrum of options to undermine NATO cohesion and target the vital interests of at least some Alliance members by either pursuing competition in the 'grey zone' or relying on emerging strategic attack options such as offensive cyber, space/anti-satellite capabilities or long-range conventional strike. In this context, while the threat of nuclear retaliation should remain a last resort and cannot be the only possible response, it contributes to deterrence by constraining the freedom of action of potential adversaries contemplating an attack against the Alliance or one of its members – which it would not be able to do if the US or the Alliance were to adopt a 'no first use' policy.

Although NATO faces various challenges in seeking to maintain a credible deterrence posture against the diversity of threats it may confront in the future, particularly issues resulting from the need for coordination and coherence among Allies, it has been adapting since 2014 to strengthen its posture and make its comparative advantages clear. For instance, even though Alliance cohesion is itself a potential target for Russia's kinetic and non-kinetic capabilities, NATO benefits greatly from having separate and independent centres of decision-making when contemplating nuclear use: the P3 (the US, the UK and France) and the North Atlantic Council itself. From a deterrence standpoint, this means that potential aggressors can never be certain that neither NATO as a whole nor any of its three nuclear-armed states would retaliate if the Alliance were under existential threat. This strategic benefit in turn confers operational advantages, as separate chains of command and control would be much harder for an adversary to suppress, disrupt or decapitate and would thus guarantee a more resilient posture. Furthermore, the existing diversity in the platforms and delivery means among the nuclear forces of the P3, in addition to the availability of NATO DCA, makes it more difficult for an adversary to develop and field countermeasures that would undermine the operational credibility of NATO's combined nuclear forces.

As a response to both the risk of fait accompli in Northeastern Europe and to the perception that the P3 countries might be unwilling to take risks to defend the Baltic and Polish Allies, NATO has established an Enhanced Forward Presence (EFP), deployed continuously since 2017. Composed of

---

[17] NATO, 'Warsaw Summit Communiqué Issued by the Heads of State and Government Participating in the Meeting of the North Atlantic Council in Warsaw, 8–9 July 2016', <https://www.nato.int/cps/en/natohq/official_texts_133169.htm>, accessed 21 January 2020.

combat units from all NATO members, particularly from the three nuclear-armed ones, the EFP greatly strengthens NATO's deterrence and defence posture, not by acting as a conventional denial force but by serving as a tripwire that would trigger the direct involvement of all Allies in the event of aggression against those countries where the EFP operates. Thus, although it is not an element of NATO's nuclear policy, one of the benefits of the EFP has been to strengthen the coherence between conventional and nuclear capabilities in the Alliance's deterrence and defence posture.

## Reducing Risks and Strengthening Stability: The Outlook for Arms Control in Europe

Arms control tends to be associated with treaty-based, legally binding constraints on nuclear and conventional capabilities. However, it was initially conceptualised as a broader and more diverse endeavour comprising formal and informal measures affecting capabilities and behaviours. In their landmark study on the topic, Thomas Schelling and Morton Halperin defined it as 'all the forms of military cooperation between potential enemies in the interest of reducing the likelihood of war, its scope and violence if it occurs, and the political and economic costs of being prepared for war'.[18]

Arms control has represented a vital concern to Allies for reasons that have persisted since the Cold War: European front-line states were, and still are, directly exposed to the consequences of escalation, formerly by the Warsaw Pact and now by Russia. The issue became important to Alliance members as soon as they grasped the dramatic costs of a nuclear exchange in Europe and the potential for a crisis to inadvertently or accidentally lead to nuclear use. Unsurprisingly, NATO therefore concerned itself with arms control as early as the 1960s, as evidenced by the 1967 Harmel report on the future tasks of the Alliance,[19] and remained directly involved in these issues both during the Cold War, as reflected by the 1979 'double-track decision' on theatre-range nuclear forces that led to the INF negotiations, and since 1989 on issues such as confidence-building measures, conventional arms control and non-strategic nuclear weapons.[20]

Although European Allies were key stakeholders in the agreements and treaties put in place to reduce the risk of war in Europe, they were not necessarily signatories to those agreements: NATO members have

[18] Thomas C Schelling and Morton H Halperin, *Strategy and Arms Control* (New York, NY: Twentieth Century Fund, 1961), p. 2.
[19] NATO, 'The Future Tasks of the'.
[20] Richard N Haass, *Beyond the INF Treaty: Arms, Arms Control, and the Atlantic Alliance* (Cambridge, MA: Center for Science and International Affairs, Harvard University, 1988).

been parties to the CFE and Open Skies treaties and to the Vienna Document on confidence-building measures, but all agreements focused on nuclear weapons – Strategic Arms Limitations Talks (SALT), INF and START – have been strictly bilateral. This occurred because the capabilities that most concerned the Soviet Union were primarily American, and also because France and the UK refused to participate in nuclear arms control negotiations with the Soviet Union due to the much smaller size of their arsenals. NATO has thus been a setting in which European Allies could voice their concerns about US policies, while the US could consult with them in advance of negotiations with Moscow or other major policy and programmatic decisions. This has helped to ensure coordination within the Alliance on issues that directly affect the security of its member states. Arms control has also represented a priority for some Allies for reasons that had less to do with strategic stability than with domestic politics and reservations regarding NATO's decision to remain a nuclear alliance, and particularly to maintain existing nuclear sharing arrangements and to modernise the DCA fleet.

While the balance of military forces in Europe has changed substantially over the past three decades, the US military remains the main provider of the Alliance's high-end capabilities (stealth fighters and bombers, long-range conventional strike, electronic warfare, air and missile defence and so forth). This, in theory, leaves European Allies poorly positioned to influence potential decisions taken by either the US or Russia. In practice, the way NATO handled the US withdrawal from the INF Treaty in 2018–19 showed that the Alliance could continue to play a useful consultative role. Since 2014, the US had formally accused Russia of violating the INF Treaty by testing and deploying a prohibited ground-launched cruise missile, the SSC-8 (9M729). President Donald Trump's announcement on 22 October 2018 that the US might soon withdraw from the Treaty looked like a somewhat unprepared and abrupt US move, but NATO ultimately succeeded in maintaining cohesion and finding a consensus view among Allies by conducting consultations, sharing intelligence and alleviating the most pressing concerns about the nature and extent of the Russian violations.[21]

As Europe and the world appear to be sliding towards a period of increased tensions between nuclear-armed powers, arms control should have an important role in channelling competition away from the riskiest

---

[21] For case studies focused on national positions of European member states on the INF crisis, see Odessa Center for Non proliferation, *Responses to the INF Treaty Crisis: The European Dimension* (Odessa: Odessa I I Mechnikov National University Press, 2019), <http://odcnp.com.ua/images/pdf/Europe-Responces-to-INF-Crisis.pdf>, accessed 21 January 2020.

behaviours. A large asymmetry persists between NATO and Russia in non-strategic nuclear weapons, as the latter's supposedly vast, modernised and diverse portfolio of capabilities stands in stark contrast to the limited number of forward-deployed US weapons. The armed forces of both Russia and NATO countries have started to integrate and deploy long-range precision and conventional strike capabilities, and the end of the INF Treaty could accelerate this process. When combined with other A2/AD capabilities (particularly anti-ship missiles and surface-to-air defences) of increasing range, as well as with electronic, cyber and space warfare assets, those systems could undermine military stability on the continent by creating incentives to strike first and offering pathways for rapid escalation.[22] In this context, NATO has remained directly involved in attempts to reduce military risks: its member states recently agreed on a package of proposals to revise the Vienna Document on confidence-building measures to increase the transparency and predictability of military practices, including of large-scale and snap exercises.[23]

Still, Russia's recent behaviour – its rhetoric, exercises and operations and particularly its attitude towards arms control agreements – will have an effect. As noted, over the past decade Russia has violated the INF Treaty, suspended its participation in the CFE Treaty, circumvented some of the obligations in the Vienna Document and failed to comply fully with the Open Skies Treaty, all the while trying to intimidate European NATO Allies. Although Russia has continued to comply with New START Treaty obligations, its past pattern of extremely selective compliance has undermined the case within the Alliance for seeking to negotiate new agreements, as Moscow's willingness to enter any substantive discussion on arms control appears questionable, at best. Russian actions have confirmed the views of those US policymakers and pundits who were already most sceptical about the benefits of arms control instruments.[24] While this attitude is unsurprising considering the growing consensus within US foreign policy circles on the need to prioritise requirements

---

[22] For an analysis of those trends and response options, see Corentin Brustlein, *The Erosion of Strategic Stability and the Future of Arms Control in Europe*, Proliferation Papers, No. 60, (Paris: Ifri, November 2018).

[23] This package was forwarded to the OSCE. See NATO, 'Speech by NATO Secretary General Stoltenberg at the High-Level NATO Conference on Arms Control and Disarmament', Brussels, 23 October 2019, <https://www.nato.int/cps/en/natohq/opinions_169930.htm?selectedLocale=en>, accessed 21 January 2020.

[24] Michaela Dodge, 'New START and the Future of U.S. National Security', The Heritage Foundation, Backgrounder No. 2407, May 2019, <https://www.heritage.org/sites/default/files/2019-05/BG3407_0.pdf>, accessed 28 January 2020; Keith B Payne and John S Foster, 'Russian Strategy: Expansion, Crisis and Conflict', *Comparative Strategy* (Vol. 36, No. 1, 2017), pp. 1–89.

associated with strategic competition with China, Russia's behaviour may also have backfired by jeopardising chances to extend the New START Treaty before its expiration in February 2021. That treaty stands out today as the last element of bilateral arms control that not only constrains the size of US and Russian strategic nuclear forces, but also provides an architecture of unique, intrusive verification and confidence-building measures. If the Treaty were to expire, the uncertainty and unpredictability surrounding the future trajectory of Russia's nuclear arsenal would dramatically increase, and thus negatively affect NATO security.[25]

## Conclusion

It remains unclear whether NATO can incentivise Russia to enter into serious talks on strategic stability in Europe in the 21st century. While NATO should not emulate Russia's behaviour simply to demonstrate a response, it must join any discussion on the future of arms control in Europe from a position of strength. Uncertainty surrounding Russia's intentions should lead Alliance members to continue strengthening NATO's deterrence and defence posture by increasing the readiness and resilience of their nuclear and conventional forces and boosting their defence spending to ensure they possess the capabilities required to deter and, if necessary, defeat aggression. They should also collectively think about the type of arms control and also confidence-building frameworks that seem best able to reduce military instability in Europe by managing the rising competition in new military capabilities such as cyber, space, autonomous systems, long-range conventional strike and electronic warfare.

---

[25] For a discussion on the uncertainties in a post-New START Treaty era, see Vince Manzo, 'Nuclear Arms Control Without a Treaty? Risks and Options After New START', Center for Naval Analyses, 2019, <https://www.cna.org/CNA_files/PDF/IRM-2019-U-019494.pdf>, accessed 21 January 2020.

# X. THE NEED FOR THE ALLIANCE TO ADAPT FURTHER

## HEINRICH BRAUSS

At their meeting in London and Watford in December 2019, the Heads of State and Government of NATO marked the 70th anniversary of the Alliance. There, they reviewed NATO's accomplishments over the past few years in adapting its strategy, military capabilities and plans across the Alliance to the evolving security environment. They also considered those challenges and threats which have become manifest since the last summit in Brussels in 2018 and which will have a bearing on the Alliance's future development.

Against this background, this chapter summarises the progress that NATO has achieved in implementing the decisions taken at the 2016 Warsaw and 2018 Brussels Summits to significantly strengthen NATO's posture. It then proposes additional measures that NATO should take to ensure its coherence and credibility in full and addresses the likely implications for the transatlantic community of the evolution of the global strategic landscape.

### The Evolving Strategic Environment

In 2014, the security environment changed fundamentally and has since continued to evolve rapidly at both a regional and global scale. For NATO, these challenges have primarily emerged from two strategic directions. To the east, Russia's aggressive actions against Ukraine and the illegal annexation of Crimea have profoundly changed the conditions for maintaining security in Europe. To the south, the 'Arc of Instability' and violence stretching across North Africa and the Middle East has fuelled terrorism and triggered mass migration, which has in turn affected the stability of Europe.

At the same time, the entire transatlantic community is challenged by the rise of China to great power status, with its growing economic, technological and military potential, and the geostrategic implications of the investment strategy and global ambitions of its autocratic regime. The growing competition among great powers – the US, China and Russia – will have a significant impact on the transatlantic partnership. For the US, China has become the key strategic competitor in trade, technology and, increasingly, military power. As a consequence, the US is shifting its strategic focus to the Asia-Pacific region, which will likely have implications for its military-strategic and operational planning, including the assignment of large portions of its military forces. This might also have implications for NATO's cohesion and effectiveness. Europe is struggling to position itself within the emerging global power structure and to make the appropriate strategic choices. Multilateral approaches to international affairs and the multinational institutions on which European security has so far been built have come under pressure. Europe's unity its and ability to operate as a coherent geopolitical actor are at stake.

All these challenges raise three interrelated questions: how should NATO cope with these concurrent challenges? How can cohesion among Allies be maintained given the US strategic reorientation? How can NATO remain relevant and credible? It is clear that the Alliance must address the implications of the evolving global power structure for Euro-Atlantic security, while retaining its focus on the immediate challenges: containing the geopolitical threat from Russia and fending off the spillover effects from instability and terrorism in the south.

## NATO's Approach to Meeting New Challenges and Threats

The summit decisions taken at Warsaw in 2016 and Brussels in 2018 set up a comprehensive strategy that focuses on achieving two goals: significantly strengthening NATO's deterrence and defence posture, and helping to project stability to increase security in its neighbourhood. Meeting these goals has mutually reinforcing effects for maintaining Alliance security.

### Projecting Stability

Crisis management and post-conflict stabilisation require a comprehensive political concept that can be tailored to specific crises or regions and combines various complementary political, economic, humanitarian and military instruments that NATO alone cannot provide. Recognising this, NATO has shifted its main effort from military interventions to assisting partners – in cooperation with other international organisations, such as the EU – to improve their resilience and provide for their own security. NATO's efforts include enhancing and deepening political dialogue with partners and offering tailored support for defence and security capacity-building, particularly to those partner countries that are located in unstable regions, such as Moldova, Ukraine, Georgia, Jordan and Tunisia. Furthermore, NATO launched a new training mission for Iraq: Allies and partners have made hundreds of trainers available for providing advice and support to the Iraqi Ministry of Defence and to several military schools and academies. NATO continues to contribute to the fight against terrorism, supporting the Global Coalition to Defeat Daesh.[1] It remains committed to ensuring long-term security and stability in Afghanistan and is continuing its Resolute Support Mission. It also sustains its engagement in Kosovo and is conducting maritime security operations in the Mediterranean under Operation *Sea Guardian*. Finally, NATO maintains its ability to intervene in regional crises with military forces, should the need arise.

*Contesting Russia's Strategy*
By its aggressive actions against Ukraine, Russia has shown that it is prepared to use force to attain geopolitical goals if it believes it can manage the associated risks. Moreover, through its military intervention in Syria, it has demonstrated its readiness to project power to regions beyond Europe, support autocratic regimes and undermine US influence. All these actions are designed to restore Russia's great power status and to achieve control over zones of influence in Russia's neighbourhood. In Europe, NATO stands in the way of this imperial concept. If its viability were undermined, Russia's expansionist efforts would gain ground.

To achieve this, Moscow is pursuing a policy of constant confrontation with the West designed to destabilise individual Allies and the Alliance as a whole. Russia's hybrid actions in peacetime aim to create confusion, uncertainty and fear within Western governments and societies.[2] Two interdependent elements are of particular concern. The first comprises Russia's efforts to achieve regional military superiority with conventional forces on NATO's borders. Rapidly deployable forces which can be massed within a few days on Russia's western border, together with diverse long-range strike capabilities to disable Alliance defences, give Moscow the option of executing a rapid, pre-emptive attack to achieve a limited land grab before NATO can react effectively. This would

---

[1]   Daesh is also known as the Islamic State of Iraq and Syria, or ISIS.
[2]   Russia's hybrid operations use a wide range of overt and covert, non-military and military means that are applied in an orchestrated way, including disinformation, malicious cyber activities and interference in national elections; subversive actions and support for separatist movements; and continued military build-up and large-scale, no-notice exercises on NATO's borders, involving nuclear elements.

be accompanied by cyber attacks, a large-scale disinformation campaign, subversive actions on Allied territories and threats to use the second element: nuclear weapons.[3] The deployment of new ground-based, intermediate-range nuclear-capable missiles has expanded Russia's significant arsenal of sub-strategic air-, sea- and ground-based nuclear forces. These missiles are capable of striking capitals and key civilian and military infrastructure in Europe, but would leave US territory unaffected – clearly signalling Moscow's aim to keep the US out of a military conflict in Europe and thus keep such a conflict geographically limited and short. As a result, in a crisis or conflict, Europe's security might be decoupled from US extended nuclear deterrence. This, in turn, might lead Moscow to believe it could paralyse NATO's decision-making and undercut Allies' determination to live up to their collective defence commitments. In this way, Russia could conclude it had achieved regional dominance, confronting NATO with a fait accompli and convincing it to stand down for fear of nuclear escalation. Such blackmail attempts through the combined use of conventional and nuclear means could disrupt NATO, thus achieving a strategic success without a long war.

As a consequence, NATO must be able to contest Russia's strategic intimidation efforts and deny Russia any options for achieving the desired political effects. To do so, NATO should pursue three primary goals: foster state and societal resilience against malicious cyber activities and disinformation; deny Russia the option of seizing territory with conventional forces in a short war; and develop measures to counter Russia's nuclear threat. NATO's current and planned activities address these goals in various ways.

## NATO's Comprehensive Long-Term Adaptation Programme

NATO efforts to strengthen its deterrence and defence and to project stability centre on achieving the ability to respond to multiple challenges and threats from several regions and across the land, air, maritime, cyber, space and nuclear domains. Moreover, NATO may have to react at short notice, perhaps simultaneously and on various scales, wherever needed across the NATO treaty area – from the North through the North Atlantic and the Atlantic Ocean, the Baltic and Black Sea regions, to the Mediterranean region, including North Africa and the Middle East.

---

[3] The 'strategy of active defence' was outlined by General Valery Gerasimov, Chief of the General Staff of the Armed Forces of Russia, in a speech to the Russian Academy of Military Science on 2 March 2019. Russia's military-strategic thinking and operational courses of action were repeatedly demonstrated by the regular large-scale *Zapad* exercises.

With a particular focus on Russia, NATO has reinvigorated the principles and key elements of deterrence, with the goal of influencing Russia's cost–benefit analysis in such a way as to discourage it from any coercion or military attack, whether because its actions might fail or because the political and military consequences would far outweigh any possible benefit and might even, in extremis, inflict unacceptable damage on itself. The Alliance must therefore be able to deter and defend against the full range of potential threats – from intimidation to a limited incursion in one region, to large-scale aggression and a nuclear threat – while recognising that, given Russia's integrated strategy, all options could involve the use of nuclear weapons.

The wide spectrum of potential threats from various geographic areas requires NATO to retain maximum awareness, flexibility and agility to ensure it has the right forces in the right place at the right time. Speedy deployment of appropriate forces to where they would be needed rather than permanent forward positioning of large forces has been the paradigm for adapting the conventional component of NATO's posture. However, for geographical reasons, there is a critical time–distance gap between a possible deployment of superior Russian forces and a build-up of substantial Alliance forces for reinforcement (discussed further in Chapter II). This applies especially to the Baltic states and Poland, which share a border with Russia, but also to other Allies that might be exposed to a Russian military threat from the sea, air and/or land, such as Norway or the Black Sea littoral states. Additionally, Russia's various anti-access/area denial (A2/AD) capabilities – such as multiple air-defence systems, long-range artillery, long-range high-precision strike capabilities and electronic warfare systems – could, in a conflict, impede or prohibit the movement of Allied forces into and across the Baltic or Black Sea regions. This creates a need for appropriate persistent forward presence of NATO multinational forces in these regions. At the same time, NATO must ensure it can execute rapid and effective reinforcement of one or more threatened Allies by deploying capable combat forces, including across the North Atlantic, where Russia is expanding its 'bastion defence' towards the Greenland–Iceland–UK (GIUK) gap.

In sum, resilience, responsiveness, readiness and rapid reinforcement are imperatives for strengthening NATO's deterrence and defence posture. They depend on rapid decision-making, maintaining sufficient forces at high readiness and the ability to move them quickly over great distances to support a threatened Ally or Allies. They also require shifting NATO's strategic mindset. In the past, out-of-area crises led to discretionary crisis response operations with long preparation times. Now, deterrence and defence – adapted to today's political and geostrategic circumstances – and the possibility of non-discretionary collective defence operations at short notice are back at the heart of Alliance strategic thinking. This requires reinvigorating a culture of readiness across the Alliance.

*Achievements to Date*

NATO has launched an ambitious programme to achieve its goals, and since 2014 has implemented a wide array of measures.[4] These have included:

- Strengthening NATO's intelligence, surveillance and reconnaissance (ISR) capabilities and accelerating its decision-making, including for short- or no-notice crises.
- Agreeing a new NATO Military Strategy, leading to a coherent concept for deterrence and defence in the whole Euro-Atlantic area and to further improving advance planning for reinforcement and defence in multiple regions.
- Enhancing the NATO Command Structure (NCS) by re-acquiring capabilities to command and control large-scale collective defence operations under hybrid warfare conditions and cyber threats. A new Cyber Operations Centre has been established and two new commands are being set up: the Joint Force Command Norfolk (JFCN) in the US, responsible for managing the movement of US and Canadian forces across the Atlantic; and the Joint Support and Enabling Command (JSEC) in Germany, in charge of enabling the movement of forces across and from Europe.
- Improving Alliance cyber defences and its ability to conduct cyber operations. This expands NATO's options and makes potential adversaries uncertain as to how NATO would respond to aggression, thus complicating adversary risk assessments and actions.
- Establishing in 2017 four Enhanced Forward Presence (EFP) multinational, combat-ready battlegroups in the Baltic states and Poland, led by the UK, Canada, Germany and the US, respectively. They demonstrate that even in the event of a limited incursion, Russia would immediately be countered by NATO as a whole, including NATO's three nuclear powers – the essence of deterrence.
- Significantly increasing the US military posture in Eastern Europe, and therefore its commitment to Europe's security, under the European Deterrence Initiative (EDI).[5] This includes the enduring presence of a US Armoured Brigade in Poland on a rotational basis. Moreover, based on a US–Polish agreement, some 1,000 additional US troops will be

---

[4] See Heinrich Brauss, 'NATO Beyond 70: Renewing a Culture of Readiness', International Centre for Defence and Security, November 2018.
[5] The EDI budget has increased from $3.4 billion in 2016 to $6.5 billion in 2019. See US Department of Defense, 'Budget Fiscal Year (FY) 2019', February 2018.

stationed in Poland, including a Divisional Headquarters (forward), while infrastructure will be established to support the rapid build-up of a US Army division.[6]

- Establishing the Multinational Divisional Headquarters South-East and the Multinational Brigade South-East in the Black Sea region, under NATO's Tailored Forward Presence (TFP), which provides the framework for regular multinational exercises in Romania and Bulgaria. NATO has also increased its naval presence in the Black Sea and conducts maritime patrol aircraft flights.

- Tripling the size of the NATO Response Force (NRF) to become a high-readiness joint force of some 40,000 troops. Its readiness has significantly increased, in particular through its spearhead force, the multinational Very High Readiness Joint Task Force (VJTF) of 5,000 troops, which is on permanent standby and ready to move its initial elements within a few days.

- Improving readiness under the NATO Readiness Initiative (NRI), whose goal by 2020 is for 30 battalions, 30 air squadrons and 30 combat vessels requiring no more than 30 days to be employed in theatre. In a second step, these forces will be developed into several land combat brigades, maritime task groups and enhanced air wings at very high readiness, thereby greatly improving NATO's military responsiveness and reinforcement capability.

- Reinforcing the Alliance Maritime Posture to cover the Atlantic Ocean and the Baltic, Black and Mediterranean Seas as a connected and coherent whole. This will improve overall maritime situational awareness, reinvigorate maritime warfighting capabilities in key areas and protect sea lines of communication, with special emphasis on the North Atlantic as a line of communication for strategic reinforcement.

- Considerably increasing NATO and individual countries' exercise activities. As an example, the joint exercise *Trident Juncture 2018* in and around Norway, involving some 50,000 soldiers from 29 Allies, Sweden and Finland, was the biggest collective defence exercise held in the past 20 years.

These are substantial achievements by any standard.

*NATO–EU Cooperation*
With both NATO and the EU confronting the same challenges and threats to Europe's security since 2014, they have enhanced their collaboration in

---

[6] See US Embassy and Consulate in Poland, 'Joint Declaration on Defense Cooperation Regarding United States Force Posture in the Republic of Poland', 12 June 2019, <https://pl.usembassy.gov/joint_declaration/>, accessed 7 February 2020.

advancing appropriate responses to an unprecedented level. Based on the Joint Declaration signed at the 2018 Brussels Summit by the NATO Secretary General and the Presidents of the European Council and the European Commission, NATO and the EU are cooperating on 74 projects in a range of areas that include countering hybrid threats and expanding cyber defence, capability development, military mobility, defence capacity building for partners and maritime security.[7]

As an example, NATO and the EU are working together to create the legal, logistical and infrastructure conditions to enable rapid movement of military forces across borders in Europe, on land and in the air, in peacetime and during crises. With regard to improving civilian infrastructure to facilitate military movements, including by heavy forces for collective defence, the European Commission plans to provide several billion euros to co-finance dual-use projects: roads, bridges, tunnels, harbours and airfields. This will also facilitate the deployment of US forces to, across and from Europe to other regions.

The EU has recently built significant momentum towards improving its capacity for civilian and military crisis response missions as part of its Common Security and Defence Policy (CSDP). While collective defence remains NATO's sole responsibility, CSDP contributes to projecting stability beyond Europe and thus to transatlantic security and burden-sharing. Furthermore, enhancing European countries' forces and capabilities benefits the Alliance and reinforces its European pillar, as 21 Allies are also EU members. Permanent Structured Cooperation (PESCO) and the European Defence Fund (EDF) help EU member states engage in enhanced multinational cooperation to develop more and better capabilities, reduce duplication, overcome fragmentation and converge their individual capability development plans over time.[8] NATO and EU staffs work together to ensure that capability development within the two organisations is complementary and the respective priorities and outputs are coherent. It is essential to ensure complete transparency and the fullest possible involvement of non-EU NATO members in EU capability projects, since they provide substantial or even indispensable

---

[7] NATO, 'Joint Declaration on EU-NATO Cooperation by the President of the European Council, the President of the European Commission, and the Secretary General of the North Atlantic Treaty Organization', 10 July 2018, <https://www.nato.int/cps/en/natohq/official_texts_156626.htm>, accessed 7 February 2020.

[8] EU member states have, to date, launched 47 cooperative projects, which cover a variety of capability areas, from a 'Euro-drone' (medium-altitude, long-endurance, remotely piloted aircraft system) to training facilities, supported by different groups of countries. See European Defence Agency, 'Current List of PESCO Projects', <https://www.eda.europa.eu/what-we-do/our-current-priorities/permanent-structured-cooperation-(PESCO)/current-list-of-pesco-projects>, accessed 7 February 2020.

contributions to Europe's security. The EU should improve its efforts in this respect; for example, due to Brexit it will now be essential to involve the UK as closely as possible in EU capability development.

## The Need for Further Adaptation

It is essential that NATO implement the decisions on how to strengthen its military posture in full and expeditiously. However, Russia's deployment of ground-based intermediate-range cruise missiles, described above, has added a new dimension to the spectrum of threats and requires NATO to take additional measures in order to maintain the coherence and credibility of its posture.

### Foster Resilience

Societal resilience to disinformation and malicious cyber activities constitutes the Allies' 'first line of defence',[9] but establishing such resilience presents a particular challenge for open, democratic societies. Allies have started to explore ways to deter an adversary from launching significant, widespread cyber attacks, for example by combining 'classic' deterrence and digital resilience and developing measures that would impose costs on the attacker. NATO must devote particular efforts to deterring hybrid threats.

### Consolidate Enhanced Forward Presence

NATO should further improve the combat readiness of the EFP battlegroups so that they become truly combined arms formations with a full set of combat, combat support and combat service support units. Furthermore, US combat units should supplement each of the battlegroups in the Baltic states, as this would further increase the deterrent value of these forces. NATO should also increase its maritime presence in the Baltic Sea to achieve sea control and secure operational depth for Alliance operations.

### Enable Joint Air Power and Joint Fires

Given the geography and space–forces–time relationship in NATO Europe, the Alliance's airpower would likely be the first-choice reinforcement force in a crisis or conflict. Joint fires, particularly with long-range precision strike and electronic warfare capabilities, are required for NATO to be able to

---

[9] See Wolf-Diether Roepke and Hasit Thankey, 'Resilience: The First Line of Defence', NATO Review, 27 February 2019, <https://www.nato.int/docu/review/articles/2019/02/27/resilience-the-first-line-of-defence/index.html>, accessed 7 February 2020.

defeat Russian A2/AD capabilities and massed forces. All relevant arrangements must be in place to ensure the rapid availability of Allied air forces, which should be visibly exercised in peacetime.

### Strengthen Air and Missile Defence
Particularly in light of the threat posed by Russian intermediate-range missiles, Allies must greatly strengthen their air and missile defences to protect critical military infrastructure and forces for reinforcement. Procuring such capabilities should become a top priority for European Allies.

### Adapt NATO's Rapid Reaction Forces
NATO should establish a number of light combat formations within the NRF that could be deployed to different regions rapidly to underpin NATO's resolve. The NRI forces should provide a high-readiness (mechanised) back-up and must therefore be vigorously developed. Follow-on forces, encompassing several larger formations, are essential to creating the Alliance's full-spectrum warfare capacity. Allies must therefore ensure timely fulfilment of their relevant NATO capability targets.

### Improve Military Mobility
In addition to the relevant NATO and EU activities, Allies that are also EU members should make every effort to accelerate EU efforts to establish the provisions required to enable military mobility across Europe. Military mobility must be exercised in peacetime, and Allies urgently need to significantly enhance their transport capacities, making them available on demand.

### Define NATO's Response to Russia's Regional Nuclear Threat
In July 2019, NATO Defence Ministers agreed on the principles for NATO's response to the regional nuclear threat posed by Russia. That response will be measured and based on a balanced, defensive package to ensure NATO's deterrence and defence posture remains credible and effective.[10] NATO insists that any employment of nuclear weapons would fundamentally alter the nature of a conflict and that its resolve and capabilities should

---

[10] See NATO, 'Press Conference by NATO Secretary General Jens Stoltenberg Following the Meetings of NATO Defence Ministers', 26 June 2019, <https://www.nato.int/cps/en/natohq/opinions_167072.htm>, accessed 7 February 2020; NATO, 'Secretary General: NATO Response to INF Treaty Demise will be Measured and Responsible', 2 August 2019, <https://www.nato.int/cps/en/natohq/news_168177.htm>, accessed 7 February 2020.

not be doubted if the security of any Ally were to be threatened. This clearly signals to Russia that any use of nuclear weapons could eventually result in unacceptable costs and should therefore not be considered.

At the same time, Allies declared they had no intention of deploying new ground-based nuclear missiles in Europe. Recognising that the Russian missiles must not be considered in isolation but in conjunction with Russia's use of conventional forces, NATO is examining a range of areas – such as ISR, air and missile defences, conventional capabilities and exercises – and ensuring a safe, secure and effective nuclear deterrent. In this context, it is essential to preserve both Alliance unity and the credibility of NATO's deterrence as a whole, including US extended nuclear deterrence. Hence, any potential solutions must contribute to maintaining the link between NATO's deterrence and defence posture in Europe and the US's strategic nuclear capability. Meanwhile, the US intends to counteract the Russian regional nuclear threat by deploying a limited number of sea-launched ballistic missiles with low-yield nuclear warheads.[11] Additionally, the US is reportedly developing a ground-based, intermediate-range, conventional precision strike weapon.[12] It could impede Russia's ability to conduct operations with conventional forces in Europe and could help to defeat its A2/AD capacity.

The response package should also include enhancing the readiness of NATO's dual-capable aircraft in addition to increasing the scale of exercises of this capability. Some of these exercises should be conducted concurrently with, or in the context of, selected conventional collective defence exercises to demonstrate the relationship between conventional defence and nuclear deterrence. Russia must realise that its own territory would not be a sanctuary if it were to threaten Europe's territory and populations with 'euro-strategic' nuclear missiles. It must be induced to embark on effective arms control as a means to enhance strategic stability in Europe and reduce risks, and it must be persuaded that this is in its own security interest.

The Alliance must therefore maintain its dual approach of strengthening both deterrence and meaningful dialogue with Russia to seek reciprocal transparency and reduce the risk of misperception and inadvertent incidents. The NATO–Russia Council should seek to facilitate mutual political understanding and predictability. It also offers an opportunity to convey clear deterrence messages.

---

[11] US Department of Defense, 'Nuclear Posture Review', February 2018, pp. 54–55.
[12] Paul Sonne, 'U.S. Military to Test Missiles Banned Under Faltering Nuclear Pact With Russia', *Washington Post*, 13 March 2019.

## Looking to the Future: Broadening the Perspective

In looking beyond Europe and its immediate neighbourhood, Allies have started to address the manifold implications of China's geopolitical strategy. At the London meeting, Allied political leaders recognised that 'China's growing influence and international policies present both opportunities and challenges that … [they] need to address together as an Alliance'.[13] This should help develop a common approach.

In this context, NATO should enhance its dialogue with partners from the Asia-Pacific region, including Japan, South Korea, Australia and New Zealand. Moreover, there are indications of an emerging Russian–Chinese entente, which could imply 'the greatest potential redefinition of worldwide power distribution in half a millennium' to the benefit of autocratic regimes that would challenge the democratic West as a whole.[14] Consequently, in strategic terms, the transatlantic community – North America and Europe together – must cope with two strategic challenges simultaneously: Russia and China. As the US shifts its strategic focus to the Indo-Pacific region, European nations will need to take far greater responsibility for the security of Europe, for NATO's deterrence and defence vis-à-vis Russia and for crisis management in the Middle East and North Africa (MENA) region. They will also need to support the US in upholding freedom of navigation, which is vital to Europe's own economies.

In addition, the disruptive technologies of the 'digital age' will profoundly change the nature of conflict in the future. Defensive and offensive cyber capabilities, new generations of sensors, space-based capabilities, autonomous weapon systems and much-improved air and missile defence will have a massive impact on security and defence and will transform the way armed forces are organised, equipped and operate.[15] NATO as a whole must invest in innovation programmes in order to maintain its technological edge and interoperability.

The totality of all these strategic challenges faced by the transatlantic partners makes equitable burden-sharing a strategic necessity. European nations must take on their full part in ensuring security for their own continent. After 20 years of focusing on crisis response missions with light,

---

[13] NATO, 'London Declaration Issued by the Heads of State and Government Participating in the Meeting of the North Atlantic Council in London, 3–4 December 2019', 4 December 2019, para. 6, <https://www.nato.int/cps/en/natohq/official_texts_171584.htm>, accessed 7 February 2020.

[14] Andrew Michta, 'As China Surges, Europe Is on the Menu', *American Interest*, September 2019.

[15] Richard Barrons, 'European Defence for the 21st Century', London School of Economics and Political Science, 2018.

deployable forces and of continuous reductions of defence budgets up to 2014, they must make vigorous efforts to restore, strengthen and transform their armed forces. This is the key rationale for all European states to increase defence expenditure, as pledged by NATO's political leaders, to at least 2% of GDP by 2024, to invest in high-end capabilities that NATO needs and to enhance contributions to operations and missions that promote NATO's and Europe's security. Fair burden-sharing is the ultimate expression of Alliance solidarity and unity and, thus, of NATO's credibility, and is essential to strengthen both the transatlantic bond and intra-European cohesion. NATO has already made progress: in 2019, nine Allies (up from three in 2014) spent at least 2% of GDP on defence while 16 Allies spent at least 20% of their defence budgets on major equipment. By the end of 2020, European Allies and Canada together will have spent some $130 billion more than they did in 2016.[16] As the central European power with the largest economic potential and the hub for reinforcement of Allies, Germany should lead by example: the readiness of the Bundeswehr is critical to the success of both NATO and EU missions.

The strategic challenges posed by Russia and China also require the EU to further enhance its contributions to transatlantic security and the defence of Europe in support of NATO's efforts. The EU should focus on supporting the development of those capabilities that are essential to the entire mission spectrum – crisis response and high-end defence alike. Improving military mobility in Europe is a case in point. Similarly, the EU member states should develop technologically advanced capabilities required to protect Europe, such as missile defence or long-range precision strike weapons, using EU instruments, for example through PESCO projects supported by the EDF. Further, European nations should establish a challenging military level of ambition for their share of NATO capabilities in quantitative and qualitative terms,[17] thereby strengthening NATO's European pillar as well as Europe's capacity to act on its own. All these endeavours would represent a significant, tangible contribution to transatlantic burden-sharing.

---

[16] See NATO, 'Defence Expenditure of NATO Countries (2013–2019)', 29 November 2019, <https://www.nato.int/cps/en/natohq/news_171356.htm>, accessed 21 January 2020.

[17] Nick Witney, 'Building Europeans' Capacity to Defend Themselves', European Council on Foreign Relations, Policy Brief 04/2019, June 2019. As the NATO Level of Ambition is defined by the 2+6 formula – that is, the pool of forces and capabilities required for NATO to be able to mount two major joint operations plus six smaller joint operations, an EU part of it could be 1+2 or 1+3.

## Conclusion

Since 2014, NATO has undergone a process of fundamental political-military reorientation and adaptation. This process will continue for the foreseeable future. The scope of the Alliance's reorientation has, however, broadened further. NATO will maintain its focus on improving Euro-Atlantic security, but will now also consider the implications for the transatlantic community of strategic developments at the global scale.

As a result, NATO faces multiple challenges. First, it must implement all the decisions taken at the recent summits to strengthen its deterrence and defence posture, in full and without delay. Second, in doing so it should take some additional measures to ensure its political cohesion, as well as the coherence and credibility of its posture to counter Russia's strategy and growing capabilities successfully. Third, it must face the implications of advanced technology for security and defence, and for the way in which Allies' armed forces will be organised and operate. Fourth, the Alliance should address the strategic implications of the evolving global power structure, in particular the rise of China, for the transatlantic partnership. To this end, NATO should strengthen its political dimension and its role as a permanent platform for Allies to discuss political, strategic and military issues of common concern and to coordinate their activities. Finally, the European Allies must take further action to strengthen the European pillar of NATO and assume a greater share of the political, military and financial burden associated with maintaining and improving their security.

These steps are essential for NATO to remain an anchor of security and stability in the Euro-Atlantic region. They are also essential for bolstering the transatlantic bond and renewing the transatlantic bargain on security. North America and Europe form a security community that defends the democratic values and institutions that autocratic powers contest. They must stand together against the multitude of strategic challenges that concern both. America needs to remain a European power, but it also needs Europe to remain the global superpower it is today – a Europe that takes on far greater international responsibility, acting as a unified, self-determined and capable partner of North America.